John:

An Eyewitness Report

DR. HAROLD J. BERRY

Originally published as *John: An Eyewitness Report* by Back to the Bible © 1976.

Copyright © 2020 by Dr. Harold J. Berry

Unless otherwise identified, all Scripture quotations in this publication are taken from the *New American Standard Bible*, © 1960, 1962, 1963, 1968, 1971, 1972, 1973, 1975, 1977, 1995 by the Lockman Foundation and are used by permission.

Loved (5.5x8.5) Self-Publishing Template © 2017 Renee Fisher [https://www.reneefisher.com]

Cover Design: © Nelly Murariu at PixBeeDesign.com

ISBN-10: 0-578-75970-5
ISBN-13: 978-0-578-75970-8

Dedication

To my two Children

Stephen Berry and Deborah (Berry) Sweazy

And through them: six grandchildren and six great-

grandchildren

I have no greater joy than this, to hear of my children

walking in the truth.   –3 John 1:4

Contents

Foreword

Welcome to the study of the Gospel of John. This is the fourth book of the New Testament. It is often recommended to inquisitive unbelievers and to new believers in Jesus as Savior. It tells what Jesus did to show Himself qualified to be the Savior of the world.

The purpose statement of the Gospel is found in chapter 20 and verses 30-31:

> **Many other signs Jesus also performed in the presence of the disciples, which are not written in this book; but these have been written so that you may believe that Jesus is the Christ, the Son of God; and that believing you may have life in His name.**

An absent person will never get closer to an actual event than to read eyewitness reports. The Apostle John is that eyewitness of the public ministry of the Lord Jesus. John is the disciple who described himself as "the one whom Jesus loved." He did not boast about his love for Jesus, but about Jesus' love for him.

Be spiritually encouraged as you read this eyewitness report.

—Dr. Harold J. Berry
Lincoln, Nebraska

Chapter 1 – God Becomes Man

THE GOSPEL OF JOHN has an important place in the Scriptures. It is an eyewitness report of what Jesus did to prove that He was the Son of God who had come to be the Savior of the world.

Although John does not identify himself by name as the writer of this Gospel, the evidence is strong from the book itself and from early Christians that he was the writer. At the conclusion of the Gospel, John mentioned "the disciple whom Jesus loved" (21:20) and said, "This is the disciple who is testifying to these things and wrote these things" (v. 24).

Purpose of This Gospel
John did not leave the reader wondering why he wrote this Gospel. The purpose is clearly stated in 20:30-31: "Therefore many other signs Jesus also performed in the presence of the disciples, which are not written in this book; but these have been written so that you may believe that Jesus is the Christ, the Son of God; and that believing you may have life in His name."

Notice several things about these verses. First, John's purpose in writing the Gospel was to present the "signs" that Jesus performed before His disciples. Second, John was selective in choosing the signs he recorded in his Gospel, for he admitted there were others that he did not record. Third, the purpose for presenting the signs was to bring others to a right relationship to Jesus Christ.

From his account, John wanted his readers to recognize

that Jesus was "the Christ," the promised Messiah, and that He was the Son of God. (The Hebrew word translated "Messiah" and the Greek word translated "Christ" have the same meaning: "anointed.") John was concerned that his eyewitness report be more than just information; he wanted readers to believe in the One he was presenting so they would have eternal life.

The Introduction

The first 18 verses of chapter 1 serve as an introduction to John's Gospel. As he wrote, John began in eternity with his statement: "In the beginning was the Word, and the Word was with God, and the Word was God. He was in the beginning with God" (vv. 1-2). Here Jesus Christ is referred to as "the Word" because He was the expression, or declaration, of God (see also v. 18). That "the Word" refers specifically to Jesus Christ is evident from verse 14: "And the Word became flesh, and dwelt among us." Verse 1 reveals that Jesus Christ was with the Father in the eternity past and emphasizes that Jesus Himself is God, for John said, "The Word was God."

John told how all things were created by Jesus Christ, and yet when He came to earth, He was rejected by the people He had created, When John said, "There came a man sent from God, whose name was John" (v. 6), he was not referring to himself. He was referring to John the Baptist who announced the coming of the Lord Jesus Christ before He appeared in His public ministry.

Concerning Christ, the Apostle John wrote, "He came to His own, and those who were His own did not receive Him" (v. 11). The first "own" in this verse refers to "His own things," and the last "own" refers to "His own people." He came to His own things—to His creation—but His own people did not receive Him. This was a reference to the nation of Israel in particular and to all people in general. The Apostle John announced good news when he said, "But as many as received Him, to them He gave the right to become children of God, even to those who believe in His name" (v. 12). Here, John closely linked receiving and believing. The one who believes in Jesus Christ in the scriptural sense of the word "believe" is the one who "receives" Him as personal Savior.

God Become Man

In his eyewitness report, John said, "The Word became flesh, and dwelt among us, and we saw His glory, glory as of the only begotten from the Father, full of grace and truth" (v. 14). This is the greatest miracle of all as far as man is concerned— God became flesh. When Jesus Christ was on earth, He was fully God and fully man; He was the God-Man. John's Gospel shows that the purpose of Christ's becoming flesh was that He might die on the cross to pay the penalty for sin so that all who receive Him as Savior might have eternal life.

Concerning Christ, John wrote, "No one has seen God at any time; the only begotten God who is in the bosom of the Father, He has explained Him" (v. 18). This verse reveals the deity of Jesus Christ, for the words literally read, "only begotten God." He Himself is God, and the words "only begotten" do not refer to His birth but to His unique position in the Godhead. Because Jesus is God, He has always existed, He was in the beginning with the Father; thus, He existed before He entered the human race by means of the virgin birth.

John the Baptist

The Apostle John continued his account by telling how John the Baptist witnessed concerning Christ. Some even thought that John the Baptist was Christ, but he explained, "I am A VOICE OF ONE CRYING IN THE WILDERNESS, 'MAKE STRAIGHT THE WAY OF THE LORD,' as Isaiah the prophet said" (v. 23). The people also asked whether he was Elijah or a special prophet God had raised up, but John the

Baptist assured them that he was neither (v. 21). The people then asked him why he was baptizing, and John explained that he was baptizing with water so that the One coming after him might be revealed to the nation of Israel (v. 31).

One day, when John saw Jesus, he let the people know He was the One of whom he spoke. John the Baptist said, "Behold the Lamb of God, who takes away the sin of the world!" (v. 29). Throughout Old Testament times, the Israelites made sacrifices, looking forward to the time when God would provide the Sacrifice to take away sin. John the Baptist let them know that Jesus Christ was the Lamb of God, the Sacrifice for sin.

Christ's First Disciple
As John the Baptist kept directing attention to Jesus Christ, people wanted to know more about Him. When two of John's disciples heard Jesus speak and asked where He lived, He said, "Come, and you will see" (v. 39). One of these men was Simon Peter's brother Andrew, who, having spent the day with Jesus, found his brother and said, "We have found the Messiah" (which translated means Christ) (v. 41).

Andrew is an example of witnessing to others concerning Christ. The believer's responsibility is to tell others about Christ and to see that they are brought face to face with their need to trust Him as Savior. Only the individual, however, can decide for himself whether or not he will receive Jesus Christ as his Savior.

When Peter was brought to Him, Jesus Gave him an Aramaic name. Jesus told Peter: "You are Simon the son of John; you shall be called Cephas" (which is translated Peter) (v. 42).

Just as Andrew told his brother about Jesus, Phillip found Nathanael and told him: "We have found Him of whom Moses in the Law and also the Prophets wrote—Jesus of Nazareth, the son of Joseph" (v. 45). From what Andrew and Philip said, it is apparent that they recognized Jesus Christ to be the fulfillment of the Old Testament promises concerning the coming Messiah.

Although Nathanael at first doubted that Jesus was the Son of God, after he met Jesus he admitted: "Rabbi, You are the Son of God; You are the King of Israel " (v. 49). Nathanael became convinced that Jesus was the Son of God when he realized that Jesus knew of him even before he came to Him (vv. 48, 50).

Jesus' First Miracle
John 2 records the first miracle that Jesus performed in his public ministry. Jesus, His mother and his disciples were invited to a wedding ceremony at Cana. During the ceremony the wine ran out, and Jesus' mother said to Him, "They have no wine" (v. 3). It is not clear from the passage whether Mary had some responsibility on this occasion and was coming to Jesus for His help or whether she was only expressing concern as a guest and wanted Jesus to do something to remedy the problem.

Whichever was the case, it was evident to Jesus that she wanted Him to do something to solve the problem because He told her: "Woman, what does that have to do with us? My hour has not yet come." (v. 4). On the surface it might seem disrespectful that Jesus called Mary "woman" instead of "mother." However, the word He used was not disrespectful. He used the same word in referring to His mother later. When he was dying on the cross, He committed her to John's care by saying, "Woman behold your son!" (19:26).

A Changed Relationship
By addressing His mother as "woman" at the beginning of His public ministry (2:4), Jesus was revealing a change of relationship. Although Mary was chosen of God for the virgin birth of Jesus, a special relationship between Him and Mary no longer existed. He had come to earth to be the Savior of the entire world. So His words of John 2:4 served as a gentle rebuke to His mother, indicating that as the Son of God He would make the choice concerning the proper time to reveal

that He had come from God. His mother then told the servants to do whatever He instructed (v. 5).

The account goes on to record that there were six stone waterpots, each holding the equivalent of 20 to 30 U.S gallons (about 75 to 115 liters). Jesus instructed that the waterpots be filled to the brim with water, and then He told the servants to draw some out and take it to "the headwaiter" (v. 8). This person was apparently in charge of the feast to make sure that everything was just right.

Between the time when the water was drawn from the waterpots and when the headwaiter ttasted it, it had been turned to wine by the miracle-working power of Jesus. This wine tasted so good it surprised the headwaiter, and he called the bridegroom and commended him for keeping the best wine until then.

There is a difference of opinion concerning whether Jesus created fermented or unfermented grape juice. However, it is important not to become so engrossed in the debate about whether it was fermented or unfermented that one misses the point of the passage, which is that Jesus performed a miracle. The Bible emphasizes this when it says, "This beginning of His signs Jesus did in Cana of Galilee, and manifested His glory, and His disciples believed in Him" (v. 11).

At Capernaum

After performing this miracle, Jesus and His followers "went down to Capernaum" (v. 12). Capernaum was northeast of Cana, but it was "down" because it was at lower altitude.

Jesus did not stay long at Capernaum because it was about time for the Jewish Passover to take place, so He "went up to Jerusalem" (v. 13). Jerusalem was south of Capernaum, but it was "up" in that it was at a higher altitude.

At the Temple

When Jesus came to the temple at Jerusalem, He discovered many abuses going on at this holy place. The Bible tells us that there were "money changers" at the temple (v. 14).

Nothing was wrong with the presence of money changers in the temple; in fact, this was needed. At the time of the Passover people would come from distances to make sacrifices and also to pay their temple tax if they had not already done so. Animals for sacrifice were made available at the temple, and those wanting to purchase the animals as well as pay their temple tax needed their currency changed into the currency used in the temple.

The sin involved seems to be that the money changers were making big profits for themselves rather than just providing a service to those who had come to worship. Jesus was so angered at this abuse that "He made a scourge of cords, and drove them all out of the temple, with the sheep and the oxen; and He poured out the coins of the money changers and overturned their tables" (v. 15).

After Jesus made such a display of power and authority, the Jews asked what sign He could show them to prove He had such authority (v. 18). Jesus responded by stating His answer in hidden form which the listeners did not understand. He said, "Destroy this temple, and in three days I will raise it up" (v. 19). Such an answer baffled the Jews, for they could not understand how Christ could rebuild the temple in three days when it had already been in building for 46 years. "But," verse 21 says, "He was speaking of the temple of His body dy." Not until after Christ had risen from the dead did His disciples understand the full significance of what He had said at this time.

Savior or Wonder-Worker?

John 2 concludes by saying, "Now when He was in Jerusalem at the Passover, during the feast, many believed in His name, observing His signs which He was doing. But Jesus, on His part, was not entrusting Himself to them, for He knew all men, and because He did not need anyone to testify concerning man, for He Himself knew what was in man" (vv. 23-25).

These verses indicate that, although they realized Jesus

was more than human in order to perform these miracles, they did not actually trust Him as personal Savior because He "was not entrusting Himself to them" (v. 24). This reveals that it is not enough just to recognize that Jesus is the Son of God; one must admit his sinful condition and personally trust Jesus Christ as his Savior. Notice also that Jesus was not at all impressed with those who were seeking signs; He is impressed only with those who believe in Him as personal Savior.

Study Questions

1. What did John say his purpose was for writing his Gospel account? (see John 20:30,31). Have you believed "that Jesus is the Christ, the Son of God"? If yes, briefly describe your salvation experience. If no, what hinders you from believing?

_____

_____

_____

_____

_____

2. Explain how John 1:18 reveals the deity of Jesus Christ. Many people today insist that, although Jesus was a good man and a great example to us—and even the son of God—He was not Himself God. How would you refute such teaching?

_____

_____

_____

_____

_____

3. In the account of Jesus' turning water into wine (John 2),
    why is it significant that He addressed His mother as
    "woman"? Was this an indication of disrespect? Why or
    why not?

_____

_____

_____

_____

4. Look at a Bible map as you read John 2:12-13. What do
    you learn concerning John's use of the directional terms
    "up" and "down" and how does that compare with the
    way we generally use those terms today?

_____

_____

_____

Chapter 2 - Why Jesus Came

AS JOHN 2 CONCLUDES, it tells of those who were following Jesus only because of the miracles He performed. Jesus did not commit Himself to them because He knew what was actually in their hearts (vv. 23-25). In contrast to these people, John 3 tells of Nicodemus. The contrast is evident in the original language (Greek) of the New Testament, because the word "but" appears in verse 1. Since there were no chapter divisions when the New Testament was written, the reader would see this contrast better because the text immediately went on to tell about Nicodemus.

While some followed Jesus only because of His miracles, Nicodemus seemed to be in a different category. He was not a believer, but he had honest questions concerning the Lord Jesus Christ to which he needed solid answers.

A Leading Pharisee
Nicodemus is referred to as "a man of the Pharisees" (3:1). The Pharisees were a strict sect of the Jews. This religious party came into existence during the years between the Old and New Testaments. The Pharisees attempted to call people back to the Mosaic Law, but

they became almost more bound by tradition than by the Law.

Not only was Nicodemus a Pharisee, he was also "a ruler of the Jews." The highest ruling body in the Jewish nation was known as the "Sanhedrin." So Nicodemus had a high position in the Jewish nation and would have been expected to be thoroughly acquainted with the Mosaic Law and with other Old Testament Scriptures which told of a coming Messiah.

A Sincere Inquirer
Nicodemus did not rely on others for information about the Lord Jesus Christ; he went directly to Jesus for answers to his questions. The Bible says that Nicodemus "came to Jesus by night" (v. 2). The Scriptures do not explain the significance of this statement. Some believe that he came to Jesus at night because he was afraid of what others would think. This is a definite possibility. However, in the Orient the custom was to visit in the cool of the evening rather than during the heat of the day. Perhaps Nicodemus came at night because he wanted to have an uninterrupted conversation with Jesus.

Whatever the reason for Nicodemus coming to Jesus by night, he told Him: "Rabbi, we know that You have come from God as a teacher; for no one can do these signs that You do unless God is with him" (v. 2). This was quite an admission for Nicodemus. He admitted that no one could do what Jesus had done without the power of God.

The Spiritual Need
When Jesus answered Nicodemus, He did not allude to his favorable remarks, but immediately spoke of a

person's need of being rightly related to God. He said, "Unless one is born again he cannot see the kingdom of God" (v. 3). Such a statement would have come as a shock to Nicodemus. After all, he had one of the most prestigious positions in the nation of Israel, but now he was being told that unless he experienced a special kind of birth he would not even be able to see God's kingdom.

Throughout the Old Testament, the Israelites looked forward to the time when God's kingdom would be established on earth. There are many prophecies related to this time, but the exact length of this kingdom is not specified in the Old Testament. The New Testament Book of the Revelation gives the length as 1000 years. (20:1-7). Inasmuch as it is 1000 years in length, the Latin word for thousand (millennium) is often used in referring to this time.

The expression "the kingdom of God" can also be used to refer to the universal kingdom of God. Every person who is in right relationship with God is in the sphere of this kingdom because he is under the rule of God. It was probably this universal kingdom to which Christ referred when He told Nicodemus that unless he was born again he could not see it.

Puzzled Nicodemus
Nicodemus did not understand Christ's words about being born again. The only birth Nicodemus knew about was physical birth, so he asked Christ: "How can a man be born when he is old? He cannot enter a second time into his mother's womb and be born, can he?" (v. 4).

Jesus responded to Nicodemus by saying, "Unless one is born of water and the Spirit he cannot enter into the kingdom of God" (v. 5). By this statement, Jesus clarified that He was not referring to a physical birth but to a spiritual birth.

"Born of Water"

There have been many differences of opinion about what Jesus meant by the words "born of water." Those who believe that water baptism is essential for salvation point to this verse as a key text. However, the Scriptures do not contradict themselves, and it is evident from other Scriptures that nothing is required for salvation in addition to believing in Jesus Christ as personal Savior. The Apostle Paul told the Philippian jailer: "Believe in the Lord Jesus, and you will be saved, you and your household" (Acts 16:31). The Philippian jailer was baptized after this time, but this was to express his salvation, not to obtain it. Further on in John 3 we read what is required for salvation, and baptism is not mentioned (vv. 15-16). Others think that the words "born of water" refer to the Word, the Bible. John 15 alludes to the cleansing power of Christ's word: "You are already clean because of the word which I have spoken to you" (v. 3).

Natural Versus Spiritual Birth

Then there are those who believe the words "born of water" refer to natural birth. They point out that the baby is sustained in its mother's womb in a sac of amniotic fluid, sometimes called "water."

Whatever Jesus wanted Nicodemus to understand by the words "born of water," verse 6 makes it clear that He was contrasting natural birth and spiritual birth. Jesus said, "That which is born of the flesh is flesh; and that which is born of the Spirit is spirit" (3:6). Jesus was telling Nicodemus that just as he had experienced birth in the physical realm, he also needed to experience birth in the spiritual realm.

The one who realizes his sinful condition and trusts Jesus Christ as his personal Savior experiences a spiritual birth. Nicodemus had experienced physical birth, but he had not yet experienced spiritual birth.

As the Lord Jesus talked to Nicodemus, He wanted him to realize that everyone needed this spiritual birth. Jesus said, "Do not be amazed that I said to you, 'You must be born again." (v. 7). "You" can be either singular or plural. So in effect, Christ was telling Nicodemus, "Don't marvel that I said to you, 'All of you must be born again.'" Not only did all Israelites, whom Nicodemus represented, need to experience this spiritual birth, but so does all mankind if they are to be delivered from condemnation.

Illustration and Explanation
To help Nicodemus understand, the Lord Jesus Christ gave an illustration from nature. The Lord told him that the wind blows where it wants to and that although you hear it, you cannot tell where it is coming from or where it is going (v. 8). Although one would know from what direction the wind is coming by feeling it on his face or by watching things being blown by it, he can also observe the results or the effects of it. When a person receives Jesus Christ as Savior, others cannot see any physical change, but there will be evident changes in a person's life.

Even after Christ's illustration, Nicodemus still did not understand. He said, "How can these things be?" (v. 9). The natural mind is not able to comprehend spiritual truths. The Bible says, "But a natural man does not accept the things of the Spirit of God, for they are foolishness to him; and he cannot understand them, because they are spiritually appraised" (1 Cor. 2:14).

Jesus asked Nicodemus: "Are you the teacher of Israel and do not understand these things?" (John 3:10). Jesus was pointing out to Nicodemus that since he was a teacher, he should know things such as this. Certainly, Nicodemus would have been expected to know about the spiritual birth that was promised to Israel in the new covenant (see Jer. 31:31-33). But Nicodemus seemed to understand only physical birth.

Look and Live
Jesus explained to Nicodemus how one experiences the spiritual birth. He said, "As Moses lifted up the serpent in the wilderness, even so must the Son of Man be lifted up; so that whoever believes will in Him have eternal life" (John 3:14-15). The Old Testament illustration of the bronze serpent on the pole, recorded in Numbers 21, emphasized that all one had to do to have salvation was to look and live. Those bitten by serpents in that Old Testament situation had only to look at the serpent on the pole and they would live.

So also, Jesus was telling Nicodemus that He would be lifted up so that all who looked on Him might have life. The one requirement for salvation is seen in John 3:15: "That whoever believes will in Him have eternal life."

This presupposes that a person realizes his sinful condition, for if he did not realize his sinful condition, there would be no need to believe in Christ as Savior. It also presupposes that a person has changed his mind about serving sin because a person who only wants to enjoy the pleasures of sin would have no interest in receiving Christ as Savior. So verse 15 is a crucial statement about what is required for salvation—believing in Jesus Christ as personal Savior.

Salvation Clear and Simple

John 3:16, which is perhaps the most familiar verse to many in all the Bible, is really an explanation of what was stated in verse 15. The word "for" at the beginning of verse 16 has the sense of "because." Having read that whoever believes in Christ will have eternal life, one might wonder, How can this be? Verse 16 explains: "For God so loved the world, that He gave His only begotten Son, that whoever believes in Him shall not perish, but have eternal life." The word "For" has the sense of "Because."

Those who believe in Christ do not perish (v. 15) because God loved the world so much He gave his only Son to pay the penalty of sin. The Scriptures abound in references to the fact that the purpose of Jesus Christ's coming to earth was to die on the cross for the sins of the world. The Bible says, "He Himself is the propitiation [satisfaction] for our sins; and not for ours only, but also for those of the whole world" (1 John 2:2). Since Christ has paid the penalty for sin, anyone who trusts in Him as personal Savior is delivered from the penalty of sin; he will not perish but has eternal life.

The words "only begotten" in John 3:16 do not mean that Jesus Christ was actually born to God. The first chapter of John makes it clear that Jesus Christ Himself is God, and as such He never had a beginning. The words "only begotten" mean "one of a kind" or "unique." Hebrews 11:17 says, "By faith Abraham, when he was tested, offered up Isaac, and he who had received the promises was offering up his only begotten son." Isaac was not Abraham's only son nor even his oldest; Ishmael was. But Isaac was Abraham's unique son.

Not to Condemn but to Save

Verses 17 and 18 reveal that Christ did not come into the world to condemn the world but to save it. He did not come to condemn the world because it was already condemned. Every person born into this world has a sin nature inherited from Adam (see Rom. 5:12). Therefore, Christ's purpose in coming into the world was to deliver from condemnation those who would believe in Him as personal Savior.

John 3:18 says, "He who believes in Him is not judged; he who does not believe has been judged already, because he has not believed in the name of the only begotten Son of God." People's love for darkness rather than light keeps them from coming to Jesus Christ (vv. 19-21).

Jesus and His Disciples

As the Apostle John continued the account of his Gospel, he said, "After these things Jesus and His disciples came into the land of Judea, and there He was spending time with them and baptizing" (v. 22). John 2:13 told of Jesus arriving at Jerusalem during the Passover. Jerusalem was the key city of Judea, and it was there that He cleansed the temple and has His conversation with Nicodemus. Now, however, Jesus and His disciples were going into other parts of Judea and baptizing those who trusted Him as Savior. The Lord Jesus Christ Himself did not actually baptize anyone; rather, His disciples baptized those who believed (4:2).

Inasmuch as Jesus and His disciples were traveling as a small band and baptizing those who received their message, this raised the question about the difference between them and John the Baptist and his disciples, who were also baptizing those who received their message. Primarily, the question was raised by the disciples of John the Baptist, who apparently were concerned because his ministry was being overshadowed by the ministry of Christ (3:25-26).

The Testimony of John the Baptist
John the Baptist explained to his disciples that he was only the forerunner of Christ, that he was like a friend (or best man) of the bridegroom who was pleased that the attention was focused on the groom (vv. 28-29). John the Baptist had no jealousy. Actually, the fact that attention was being focused on Christ indicated John the Baptist had done his work well as a forerunner of Christ.

The testimony of John the Baptist is summed up in his words: "He must increase, but I must decrease" (v. 30). Now that Jesus was on the scene in His public ministry, John the Baptist realized it was important that the attention be shifted from himself to Jesus Christ. John the Baptist said concerning Christ: "For He whom God has sent speaks the words of God; for He gives the Spirit without measure" (v. 34). John 1:1 spoke of Christ as the "Word," which refers to the fact that He was the expression of God. John 3:34 reveals that Christ spoke the words of God. There was no limit to the Spirit's power in the life of Christ, as is indicted by the words "For He [God] gives the Spirit without measure."

A Remarkable Contrast
John 3 is a great chapter on the subject of believing in Christ as Savior, and it concludes with the statement, "He who believes in the Son has eternal life; but he who

does not obey the Son will not see life, but the wrath of God abides on him" (v. 36). Notice the contrast! The one who trusts Jesus Christ as Savior has eternal life, but the one who rejects Jesus Christ as Savior has only the wrath of God on him. Which side of this contrast each person is on depends on the personal choice he makes concerning Christ. If you have not trusted Christ as your personal Savior, it is important that you do so before it is eternally too late.

Study Questions

1. What is significant about the fact that Nicodemus went directly to Jesus for information rather than relying on what others said about Him? Where do you go to learn about God and about the Scriptures?

_____

_____

_____

_____

_____

2. Why did Jesus' Words about being born again puzzle Nicodemus? Now explain the concept of being "born again" to someone who had never heard it before?

_____

_____

_____

_____

_____

3. In what way is spiritual birth like the wind?

_____

_____

_____

_____

_____

4. What relationship did "the serpent in the wilderness" have to Jesus' life and ministry?

_____

_____

_____

_____

_____

5. Some people teach that the words "only begotten" in John 3:16 indicate that Jesus was created and thus He is not God. How would you refute this teaching?

_____

_____

_____

_____

_____

6. Do you have eternal life? How can you be sure?

_____

_____

_____

_____

_____

_____

_____

Chapter 3 – Jesus' Concern for All People

BECAUSE CONFUSION HAD ARISEN concerning the ministries of John the Baptist and the Lord Jesus Christ, Jesus decided to leave Judaea for Galilee. The Bible says: "Therefore when the Lord knew that the Pharisees had heard that Jesus was making and baptizing more disciples than John (although Jesus Himself was not baptizing, but His disciples were), He left Judea and went away again into Galilee" (John 4:1-3).

John the Baptist had been a faithful forerunner, and apparently the Lord did not want to add to the confusion concerning the distinction of their specific ministries, so He chose to go to another location. Since His disciples did the baptizing, no one could boast that he had been baptized by Christ.

Jesus in Samaria
The region of Galilee was north of Judea and was separated from it by a territory known as Samaria. For centuries there had been hostile feelings between the Samaritans and the Jews. This animosity stemmed back to the time when the ten tribes of Israel, which formed the Northern Kingdom, were taken captive by Assyria. "The King of Assyria brought men from Babylon, and from Cuthah, and from Avva, and from Hamath, and from Sepharvaim, and settled them in the cities of Samaria in place of the sons of Israel. So they possessed Samaria and lived in its cities" (2 Kings 17:24) As a result of

this mixing of nationalities, the Samaritans were not of full Jewish blood; therefore, they were looked on with scorn by the Jews of Judea.

The bitter feelings between these two groups were still strong during the time when Christ was on earth. So a Jew who wanted to go from Judea to Galilee would usually cross to the east side of the Jordan River to avoid going through Samaria. So it was a very significant statement for the Bible to record that Christ "had to pass through Samaria" (John 4:4). The Lord Jesus Christ did not shun any group, and His action at this time demonstrated that clearly.

The Weary Savior
While passing through Samaria, Jesus became weary and sat by a well known as "Jacob's well" (v. 6). The fact that Jesus became weary reveals that even though He was completely God, He was also completely man. He experienced tiredness, and the following verses reveal that He experienced thirst. Although He was completely man as well as completely God, Jesus Christ was not born with a sin nature as all others have been.

The disciples had gone into the nearby city to buy food, and while the Lord was sitting on the well, a woman came to draw water. He asked her to give Him a drink (v. 7), and she was shocked that He would make such a request of her. Her reply to Him reveals the deep feelings of animosity between the Jews and the Samaritans. She said to Him, "How is it that You, being a Jew, ask me for a drink since I am a Samaritan woman?" (For Jews have no dealings with Samaritans) (v. 9).

Notice that the woman referred to Jesus Christ as "a Jew." Although He had always existed because He was God, Jesus Christ was born into the human race through the Jewish nation. It is evident that He had the physical characteristics of a Jew, or else the Samaritan woman would not have made such a statement.

Living Water

Jesus responded that if she realized who was speaking to her, she would have asked Him for water, and He would have given her "living water" (v. 10). She could not understand what He meant by such a statement because He did not have any container with which to draw water. She asked Him, "You are not greater than our father Jacob, are You, who gave us the well?" (v. 12).

Jesus was seeking to teach her spiritual truths by drawing an analogy to the water she was so concerned about. Therefore He said, "Everyone who drinks of this water will thirst again; but whoever drinks of the water that I will give him shall never thirst" (vv. 13-14).

Now the woman became definitely interested. One can imagine how many times she had come to the well to laboriously draw water, and this stranger offered a cup of water that would quench thirst forever! She responded by saying, "Sir, give me this water, so I will not be thirsty nor come all the way here to draw" (v. 15).

Without commenting any more about water, the Lord Jesus told her to go and bring her husband to Him (v. 16). She answered, "I have no husband" (v. 17), and then He revealed that He knew all about her, for He said, "You have had five husbands, and the one whom you now have is not your husband" (v. 18). The woman was impressed by this display of knowledge and knew she was talking to someone far above average. She said, "Sir, I perceive that You are a prophet" (v. 19).

About Worship

The woman focused attention on a significant difference between the worship of the Samaritans and the worship of the Jews, saying, "Our fathers worshiped in this mountain, and you people say that in Jerusalem is the place where men ought to worship" (v. 20). It is not recorded that Jesus actually said these words; she may have assumed that because He was a Jew He would maintain that everyone should worship in Jerusalem.

The Samaritans had their own temple at mount Gerizim, and the Jews had their own temple at Jerusalem. Jesus made clear the time was coming, and actually was here, when people would not worship at a specific geographical location (v. 21). He referred to all Samaritans when he said, "You worship what you do not know; we worship what we know, for salvation is from the Jews (v. 22). The Lord did not condone the false worship of the Samaritans, because God had not been revealed through them but through the nation of Israel.

"Salvation is from the Jews" (v. 22) in that God gave the Scriptures by means of the Jews, and Jesus Christ Himself was born of the Jewish nation. He came to provide not only for their salvation but also for the salvation of the entire world.

True Worship
Jesus revealed that true worship was not associated with geographical location of nationality when He said, "But an hour is coming, and now is, when the true worshipers will worship the Father in spirit and truth; for such people the Father seeks to be His worshipers. God is spirit, and those who worship Him must worship in spirit and truth" (vv. 23-24).

Notice that the words "in spirit and truth" occur in each of these verses. Jesus was emphasizing to the woman that worship no longer necessarily involved a particular building, such as a temple. Many today talk about worshiping God, but they do not believe the right things about Him. It is impossible to really worship God unless one agrees with what God has said about Himself.

The Scriptures are God's written revelation concerning Himself, so the one who worships in "truth" must believe what the Scriptures say. Just as the Samaritans were claiming to worship God and yet were involved in heretical practices, some today claim to worship God, but they do not believe that Jesus Christ was born of a virgin, or that He is God, or that He has risen from the dead, and that He will personally return. Any worship of God that does not agree with what God has said about Himself is not according to the "truth." Remember that Jesus Himself said, "I am the way, and the truth, and the life; no one comes to the Father but through Me" (John 14:6).

Realization and Evangelization

The woman of Samaria told the Lord she knew that when the Messiah came, He would tell them all things (v. 25). Jesus replied: "I who speak to you am He" (v. 26). What a shock this must have been to the woman! At that point, the disciples returned from the city and interrupted the conversation. They were amazed that Christ was speaking with the woman, but no one asked Him why.

The woman returned to the city and told the people, "Come, see a man who told me all the things that I have done; this is not the Christ, is it?" (v. 29). According to the Greek language in which the Apostle John originally wrote this account, the woman phrased her question in a way that indicated she expected the answer no. It is thought that perhaps she stated her question in this way to arouse curiosity, whereas to have made the bold assertion that Jesus was the Christ may have caused antagonism. Whatever the reason, she aroused the curiosity of the people to the extent that they left the city to see this person.

Puzzled Disciples

Meanwhile, the disciples were still trying to figure things out. They had brought food and had encouraged Jesus to eat, but he had refused saying, "I have food to eat that you do not know about" (v. 32). The disciples did not understand this statement and wondered if someone else had given Him food to eat, but Jesus said to them: "My food is to do the will of

Him who sent Me and to accomplish His work" (v. 34).

Jesus then drew an analogy to point out to the disciples the urgency of getting the gospel to everyone. He said, "Do you not say, 'There are yet four months, and then comes the harvest'? Behold, I say to you, lift up your eyes and look on the fields, that they are white for harvest" (v. 35). Jesus was concerned about a spiritual harvest and wanted to make His disciples aware of the urgency. He did not want to be concerned about food while many were on the way to visit Him because of the testimony of the Samaritan woman.

The Bible says, "From that city many of the Samaritans believed in Him because of the word of the woman who testified, "He told me all the things that I have done" (v. 39). They asked Jesus to stay with them and He spent two days there before leaving for Galilee.

Into Galilee

Verse 44 states "For Jesus Himself testified that a prophet has no honor in his own country." Normally, this statement is taken to mean that it was disappointing that more honor wasn't given to Jesus; yet, in its context we see that He wanted to go to Galilee (His home area) because a prophet is without honor in his own country. In Judea, from which He had recently come, there was much debate about Him, and this hindered His doing the kind of work He really wanted to do. So it was an advantage to Him to be in Galilee, in His own country, where this kind of attention would not be focused on Him, as is indicated by verse 45: "So when He came to Galilee, the Galileans received Him, having seen all the things that He did in Jerusalem at the feast; for they themselves also went to the feast."

At Cana Again

When Jesus came to Cana in Galilee, He was met by an official whose son was at the point of death. The official urged Jesus to come to his house to heal his son, but Jesus refused saying, "Go; your son lives." (v. 50). The same verse

says, "The man believed the word that Jesus spoke to him."
When the official arrived at home the next day, he learned that
the fever had left his son on the preceding day at the time
when Jesus had promised his son would live" (vv. 50, 53).

The Apostle John then specifically stated, "This is again a
second sign that Jesus performed when He had come out of
Judea into Galilee" (v. 54). The first miracle to which John
referred is recorded in chapter 2 and involved turning water
into wine. Jesus had performed other miracles in Judea (2:23),
but the healing of the official's son was the second miracle He
had performed in Galilee.

Healing at the Pool
In writing his Gospel, John does not specify how long Jesus
spent in Galilee at this time, but he says, "After these things
there was a feast of the Jews; and Jesus went up to Jerusalem"
(5:1). While there, Jesus met a person by a pool who had been
sick for 38 years. When Jesus saw him, He asked, "Do you
wish to get well?" (v. 6). The man answered Him: "Sir, I have
no man to put me into the pool when the water is stirred up,
but while I am coming, another steps down before me" (v. 7).
Without responding to his comments about the pool, Jesus
said to him: "Sir, I have no man to put me into the pool when
the water is stirred up, but while I am coming, another steps
down before me" (v. 8). The Jews were greatly disturbed,
however, when they saw this man carrying his bed on the
Sabbath (vv. 9-10).

It is interesting to note that the sick man was not a believer
in Jesus Christ as his personal Savior at the time he was
healed. In fact, he did not even know who had healed him.
When the Jews asked who it was, he wasn't able to tell them.
Later Jesus met the same man in the temple and revealed
Himself to him (v. 14). When the man left the temple, he told
the Jews who had healed him, and their hatred of Jesus
became even more intense. Not only did they persecute Jesus
(v. 16), but they "were seeking all the more to kill Him,
because He not only was breaking the Sabbath, but also was

calling God His own Father, making Himself equal with God." (v. 18).

Jesus Equal With the Father
Some say that Jesus was not God, and they refer to the words "Father" and "Son" as indicating that Jesus is not equal to God. Yet the Jews clearly understood that Jesus was claiming to be equal with God, and this is why they sought to kill Him. Had He only been claiming an inferior position to God, they would not have been nearly so disturbed.

That Jesus is equal with the Father is also seen in that the same honor is to be given to each: "He who does not honor the Son does not honor the Father who sent Him" (v. 23). On the basis of these words, the person who does not properly honor Jesus Christ by recognizing Him to be equal with the Father is not properly honoring the Father either.

Great Assurance
Christ gave a great promise concerning salvation when He said, "He who hears My word, and believes Him who sent Me, has eternal life, and does not come into judgment, but has passed out of death into life" (v. 24). What a tremendous verse of assurance! Any person who has trusted Jesus Christ as his personal Savior may count on the fact that he has eternal life and will never come under commendation!

To doubt this is to doubt God's word—which is to doubt God Himself. Hebrews 6:18 says it is "impossible for God to lie." However, it is a sobering thought to remember that the person who has not trusted Jesus Christ as Savior is already under judgment (John 3:18).

Two Resurrections
Jesus referred to two kinds of resurrection when He said: "Do not marvel at this; for an hour is coming, in which all who are in the tombs will hear His voice, and will come forth; those who did the good deeds to a resurrection of life, those who committed the evil deeds to a resurrection of judgment" (5:28-

29). Although both resurrections are mentioned in these verses, nothing is said about whether or not the resurrections take place at the same time.

The Book of Revelation reveals that the two resurrections are separated by at least 1000 years. There are various resurrections of believers. For example, the resurrection of the dead in Christ at the Rapture (John 11:25; I Cor. 15:51-54; I Thess. 4:16) and the resurrection of martyred Tribulation saints (Rev. 6:9; 7:4-14). These are all part of the first resurrection and take place before the 1000-year rule of Christ (the Millennium). Unbelievers will be resurrected after the 1000-year rule of Christ to stand before the Great White Throne Judgment, and will then be cast into the lake of fire because they have not trusted God for salvation (Rev. 20:11-15). The decision that each person makes about Jesus Christ determines which resurrection he will take part in. This is why it is important to receive Jesus Christ as personal Savior before it is eternally too late. No opportunity is given after death to trust Christ as Savior and escape condemnation. Hebrews 9:27 says, "It is appointed for men to die once and after this comes judgment."

Witnesses to Christ
The concluding portion of John 5 tells of the witnesses to Jesus Christ. Jesus said, "If I alone testify about Myself, My testimony is not true" (v. 31). Everything was to be confirmed by at least two or three witnesses. Jesus was acknowledging that if only one person said something, his testimony would be doubted.

Jesus gave four witnesses concerning Himself that revealed what He said was true: John the Baptist (vv. 33-35), His works (v. 36), the Heavenly Father (vv. 37-38), and the Scriptures (vv. 39-47).

Concerning John the Baptist, Jesus said, "He was the lamp that was burning and was shining and you were willing to rejoice for a while in his light" (v. 35). In this statement Jesus was pinpointing the fact that although they had accepted the one who was preparing the way for the King, they had not accepted the King Himself.

Concerning His own works, Jesus said, "But the testimony which I have is greater than the testimony of John; for the works which the Father has given Me to accomplish—the very works that I do—testify about Me, that the Father has sent Me." (v. 36). The miracles Jesus performed were supernatural beyond question. Even Nicodemus was forced to admit: "Rabbi, we know that You have come from God as a teacher; for no one can do these signs that You do unless God is with him" (3:2). Remember that John's purpose in writing his Gospel was to tell of some of the miracles that Jesus performed (20:30-31).

Concerning the witness of the Father, Jesus pointed out to the Jews that He had been sent by the Father, but they did not receive the One whom the Father had sent (5:37-38). Thus, Jesus was telling the Jews that they really did not honor God or else they would accept the One whom He had sent.

Concerning the witness of the Scriptures, Jesus referred the Jews to what Moses had written and said, "For if you believed Moses, you would believe Me, for he wrote about Me" (v. 46). Jesus was referring to statements by Moses recorded in such verses as Genesis 3:15; 12:3; 49:10 and Deuteronomy 18:15, which all found their fulfillment in the Lord Jesus Christ. To His Jewish listeners who claimed to strictly follow the writings of Moses, Christ said, "But if you do not believe his writings, how will you believe My words?" (John 5:47).

The refusal of the Jews to receive Him as the Messiah was pointed out by Christ to be actually a refusal to believe what Moses had written in the first five books of the Old Testament. This indicates that the 66 books of the Bible are a single unit and that an individual is not free to accept some of the teachings of those books and not others. God meant for us to diligently study His entire revelation so we would know the message that He wants to convey to us.

Study Questions

1. In what way did the Jews typically demonstrate their feelings toward the Samaritans? How did Jesus' behavior contrast with what was generally accepted? What types of people do you tend to avoid? Why?

_____

_____

_____

_____

_____

2. What was the Samaritan woman's misconception about worship? In your own words, define worship. What does it mean to worship "in spirit and in truth"?

_____

_____

_____

_____

_____

3. What was the result of the Samaritan woman's testimony to her neighbors? What actions and activities of yours turn the thoughts of your neighbors to Jesus Christ? What can

you do to witness more effectively?

_____

_____

_____

_____

_____

4. What did Jesus claim about Himself that incensed the Jews? Some religious groups today insist that just because Jesus was the Son of God, that did not make Him equal with God. How do you know this assertion is false?

_____

_____

_____

_____

5. The lesson mentions two resurrections. In which one will you take part? How do you know?

_____

_____

_____

_____

_____

6. List the four witnesses concerning Himself that Jesus
   mentioned in John 5. Explain how each one testified of
   Jesus.

_____

_____

_____

_____

_____

_____

_____

_____

_____

_____

Chapter 4 – Jesus, the Bread of Life

AFTER THE EVENTS RECORDED in John 5, "Jesus went away to the other side of the Sea of Galilee (or Tiberias)." (6:1). Because of the miracles He had performed, some people made a habit of following Him wherever He went (v. 2).

Although there was almost always a crowd around Him, Jesus was concerned to spend time with His disciples as well as time alone in prayer. So we're told that He "went up on the mountain, and there He sat down with His disciples" (v. 3). Imagine all that they may have discussed as they were alone on the mountain in this precious time of fellowship and learning!

Jesus' Question

Jesus saw a crowd coming to Him, so he asked Phillip a question that tested his faith: "Where are we to buy bread, so that these may eat?" (v. 5). That Jesus said this to test Philip is seen from verse 6: "This He was saying to test him, for He Himself knew what He was intending to do." This reveals the principle that sometimes God allows certain circumstances to cause us to see the need of depending on Him completely. God knows the solution to the problem, but He wants us to admit that we see no solution and to be willing to rely entirely on Him.

Although Jesus had asked where they might buy bread, Philip was particularly concerned about what it would cost to buy enough food even if it could be found. The cost Philip estimated it would take to buy that amount of food was approximately 200 day's wages at that time (v. 7).

Helpless Disciples

That the other disciples knew of the question that had been posed to Phillip was evidenced by the fact that Andrew said, "There is a lad here who has five barley loaves and two fish, but what are these for so many people?" (v. 9). The "loaves" to which Andrew referred were small barley cakes, not nearly the size of modern-day loaves of bread. The disciples were completely inadequate to solve the problem faced by the hungry multitude, and it was at that time that Jesus gave instructions to have the people sit down (v. 10).

Here again we see a principle—God usually does not work until believers admit they are unable to solve the problem themselves. As long as Christians think they have a solution, there is no need for them to rely on God. God is able to get the glory only as Christians realize they don't have the answers and must rely on God to work according to His will.

Feeding the Multitude

John recorded the fact that there were "about five thousand" present (v. 10). It was not the custom to count the women and children; therefore, the total number would have been much higher than 5,000.

When the people had sat down, Jesus took the barley cakes and fishes, distributed them to the disciples, and the disciples distributed them to the people. Then they all ate until they were filled (vv. 11-12). Not only was there enough food to feed all of the people, but there were also 12 baskets of leftover fragments that the disciples collected afterwards (v. 13).

Response of the People

Notice the response of the people after they saw the miracle that Jesus performed. They said, "This is truly the Prophet who is to come into the world" (v 14). They were probably remembering the statements of such passages as Deuteronomy 18:15, where Moses wrote: "The LORD your God will raise up for you a prophet like me from among you, from your countrymen, you shall listen to him.."

From John 6:14 it is evident that the people recognized Jesus as the fulfillment of this one that had been prophesied in the Old Testament; yet the succeeding verses of chapter 6 reveal that, although they were interested in what He could do for them physically, they were not interested in what He could do for them spiritually. Because Jesus had taken care of their hunger, they wanted to make Him king, even if they had to do it by force, so Jesus left the crowd and went to a mountain to be by Himself (v. 15).

On the Sea of Galilee
That evening the disciples came down to the shore of the Sea of Galilee, boarded a boat and headed for Capernaum (vv. 16-17). The sea of Galilee was about 7 miles wide and 12 miles long, so it would be quite the trip across it. And it was not unusual for strong west winds to blow in from the Mediterranean Sea and make the waters of Galilee extremely turbulent.

After the disciples had rowed about three or four miles, a strong wind came up (vv. 18-19) which endangered their lives. They then saw Someone walking on the sea coming toward them. This really frightened them, but then He spoke and said, "It is I; do not be afraid" (v. 20). What a relief! It was Jesus.

It is possible that the reason Jesus came to them in this miraculous manner was to assure His small band of disciples that their belief in Him as the Messiah was well founded, even though the large crowd had followed Him only because He had filled their stomachs. The disciples "were willing to receive Him into the boat, and immediately the boat was at the land to which they were going" (v. 21).

Some claim that the boat was miraculously transported in

an instant to their destination on the shore. Such an interpretation is possible, but it may also mean that the fellowship the disciples had with the Lord was so precious that the trip seemed to go by quickly. Either view would be acceptable without violating the text.

The Seeking Crowd

The crowd back on the other side of the lake was dumbfounded the next day when they came to the shore. They apparently knew that the disciples had taken the only boat, and now Jesus was gone, and there was no explanation of how He got away (v. 22). When some boats came by, the people boarded them and crossed the sea to Capernaum to see if Jesus was there (v. 24). They found Him and asked when He had come there (v. 25). Rather than answering their specific question, He said: "Truly, truly, I say to you, you seek Me, not because you saw signs, but because you ate of the loaves and were filled" (v. 26).

The purpose of the miracles was to reveal that Jesus Christ was indeed the Son of God. So if one really believed the miracles and their intent, he would have to admit that Jesus was the Son of God. These people were far from being willing to admit this.

Jesus told them: "Do not work for the food which perishes, but for the food which endures to eternal life, which the Son of Man will give to you, for on Him the Father, God, has set His seal" (v. 27). To His statement that they ought to labor, or work, they responded: "What shall we do, so that we might work the works of God?" (v. 28).

These people had the popular concept that one merits position before God by what he is able to do. Jesus showed how wrong they were when He said: "This is the work of God, that you believe in Him whom He has sent" (v. 29). These people wanted to do something to be right with God, and Jesus told them the only thing they could do was to believe in Him. One never receives salvation by works but by grace through faith in Christ. The Apostle Paul said it in these words: "For by grace you have been saved through faith; and that not of yourselves, it is the gift of God; not as a result of works, so that no one may boast" (Eph. 2:8-9).

When they heard the statement of Jesus that they should believe in Him, the people asked what sign He would perform for them so they might believe Him (John 6:30). Remember, this was the same crowd that had been fed by him on the other side of the Sea of Galilee. They just witnessed a great miracle by the lord Jesus Christ, yet they wanted Him to do something else that would be miraculous. They referred to the time of Moses when the Israelites received bread from heaven to eat (v. 31).

Bread From Heaven

Jesus explained to the crowd that the bread He was able to give had some similarity to the Old Testament manna, but it also had some significant differences. The similarity was that both originated with God. Jesus said, "Truly, truly, I say to you, it is not Moses who has given you the bread out of heaven, but it is My Father who gives you the true bread out of heaven" (v. 32).

Jesus explained what the true bread from heaven was when He said: "For the bread of God is that which comes down out of heaven, and gives life to the world" (v. 33). This was a key distinction between the true bread from heaven and the Old Testament manna. The Old Testament manna kept people alive, but it could not give life. When the people were offered something that could give life, they responded just like the woman at the well, saying, "Lord, always give us this bread" (v. 34). Their attention was still on the physical, not on the spiritual.

The True Bread of Life

Jesus then revealed who the true bread is when He said, "I am the bread of life" (v. 35). He added: "He who comes to Me will not hunger, and he who believes in Me will never thirst" (v. 35) He was well aware that the people had not really believed in Him as a deliverer from sin, for He told them: "you have seen Me, and yet do not believe" (v. 36). This verse reveals that believing involves more than just recognizing that Jesus lived at a point in history. These people knew the historic fact, but Jesus described them as ones who "do not believe." They did not recognize their sinful condition and trust Jesus Christ as Savior, or Deliverer from their sins.

Concerning salvation, Jesus said: "All that the Father gives Me will come to Me, and the one who comes to Me I will certainly not cast out" (v. 37). What a tremendous verse! Any who desire to come to Jesus Christ can do so, and He has promised not to turn anyone away.

Manna and Living Bread

Jesus made other statements concerning salvation, but what troubled the Jews the most was that He had said, "I am the bread that came down out of heaven" (v. 41). They could not understand why He could say this. They knew His family, which was sufficient evidence to them that He had not come down out of heaven (v. 42).

Although the people were murmuring against Him, Jesus told them, "He who believes has eternal life" (v. 47). Jesus then repeated what He had said earlier, "I am the bread of life" (v. 48).

Having said this, Jesus pointed out to them that their ancestors who ate manna in the wilderness were dead, but whoever would eat of the bread of life would not die (vv. 49-50). This was clearly putting Himself on a higher level than Moses, and the Jews never appreciated anyone who did that. Jesus said further, "I am the living bread that came down out of heaven; if anyone eats of this bread, he will live forever; and the bread also which I will give for the life of the world is My flesh" (v. 51).

Confused Hearers

This was about all the Jews could take. They found it impossible to understand how Jesus could give them His flesh to eat (v. 52). He added to their frustration when He said, "Truly, truly, I say to you, unless you eat the flesh of the Son of Man and drink His blood, you have no life in yourselves" (v. 53). No doubt the Jews thought it was bad enough that He had talked about eating His flesh, but now He had the audacity to suggest they must drink His blood. Throughout the Old Testament, it was emphasized to the Jews that they were not to eat blood (see Lev. 17:11-12), and now, they thought, this Person was telling them they should violate the Old Testament Scriptures!

Jesus drove His point home even harder. He said, "He who eats My flesh and drinks My blood has eternal life, and I will raise him up on the last day" (John 6:54).

Partaking of Christ

Jesus was not referring to actually eating His flesh and drinking His blood; He was not suggesting cannibalism. Also He was referring to something they could do while He was alive that would give them eternal life, so His words meant something different than actually eating His flesh and drinking His blood. Just as the Israelites in the Old Testament had to assimilate the manna in order to be nourished by it, one must believe on, or assimilate, Jesus Christ in order to benefit from him. Earlier, He had told this same group that the only thing they could do to have eternal life was to "believe on Him" (v. 29).

It is evident from John 6 that Christ was emphasizing that the eating of His flesh and the drinking of his blood had to do with believing in Him. It was necessary for Jesus to become flesh and blood in order that He might come to earth and die on the cross for the sin of the world (Heb. 2:14). When a person believes in Jesus Christ as his personal Savior, he benefits from the flesh and blood that Jesus Christ took on Himself.

John 6:59 reveals where Jesus was when He discussed these things with the Jews: "These things He said in the synagogue as He taught in Capernaum."

Not Really Believers

What Jesus had said was impossible for the Jews to accept. "Therefore many of His disciples, when they heard this said, "This is a difficult statement; who can listen to it?" (v. 60). From this verse we see that the word "disciples" did not always mean "believers." Usually it is used of believers, but a disciple is simply one who learns. These people had been following Jesus to learn of Him, but it was evident from what they said that they had never trusted Him as personal Savior.

Jesus explains that He was referring to something beyond the physical realm when He said, "It is the Spirit who gives life; the flesh profits nothing; the words that I have spoken to you are spirit and are life" (v. 63). Again, He emphasized to the people, "There are some of you who do not believe" (v. 64). The verse goes on to explain, "For Jesus knew from the beginning who they were who did not believe, and who it was that would betray Him" Jesus was able to see into the hearts of individuals and know who believed in Him as Savior and who did not. He was also aware of which disciple would betray Him.

The effect that Jesus' statements had on the crowd is evident from verse 66: "As a result of this many of His disciples withdrew and were not walking with Him anymore." As previously pointed out, the word "disciples" does not necessarily mean "believers." This chapter of John's Gospel shows that these people were following Him only for the physical benefits, not for spiritual ones.

Jesus and the Twelve

After the crowd had gone away, Jesus turned His attention to the small band of men he had chosen. They were referred to as "the twelve" in verse 67, which records Christ's question to them: "You do not want to go away also, do you?" At this point Peter spoke for the group: "Lord, to whom shall we go? You have words of eternal life. We have believed and have come to know that You are the Holy One of God" (vv. 68-69).

Peter and the other disciples did not understand many

things, but they knew that their hope was only in Jesus Christ. It is good for every believer to remember that when he is faced with circumstances he cannot possibly understand. God is still on the throne and knows what He is doing.

After these reassuring words of Peter, Jesus says, "Did I Myself not choose you, the twelve, and yet one of you is a devil?" (v. 70). Verse 71 makes it clear to whom Jesus was referring: "Now He meant Judas the son of Simon Iscariot, for he, one of the twelve, was going to betray Him." Although Judas was not the Devil himself, he was serving the Devil because he had never received Christ as his Savior.

Study Questions

1. Why did Jesus ask Philip where they could get enough bread to feed the multitude? Recall a time when you saw no solution to a problem you were facing, and explain how God worked in that situation.

_____

_____

_____

_____

2. What was the response of the people after Jesus performed the miracle of the loaves and fishes? Why did Jesus leave the crowd to go by Himself to a mountain?

_____

_____

_____

_____

_____

3. What was the purpose of Jesus' miracles? In spite of the miracle they had witnessed the day before, what did the people ask Jesus for in John 6:30? What was HIs response? Have you ever asked God to give you a sign to help you believe in Him? Why did you think you needed a sign?

_____

_____

_____

_____

4. Even though the people had been fed by Jesus and knew He had performed a miracle, Jesus told them they did not really believe. Why did He say this? What word pictures did He then use that turned the Jews against Him? Why were they angered by His statements? In your own words, explain what Jesus meant with His use of those word pictures.

_____

_____

_____

_____

_____

5. What did Peter's words at the end of John 6 reveal? What
    does Peter's declaration mean to you personally?

_____

_____

_____

_____

_____

_____

_____

_____

_____

_____

Chapter 5 – Jesus Disbelieved and Hated

HAVE YOU EVER WONDERED what Jesus' own family thought about Him? Were the Jews ever able to trap Jesus by their questions? John 7 and 8 give the answers to these questions.

After the events recorded in John 6, "After these things Jesus was walking in Galilee, for He was unwilling to walk in Judea because the Jews were seeking to kill Him" (7:1). The Jews were so hostile against Jesus that He decided to avoid Judea as much as possible. But then came the time for the Feast of Tabernacles (v. 2), and Jews would be expected to go to Jerusalem at this time. What would Jesus do?

Disbelieved by His Own Family
Those in His own family urged Jesus to go to Judea and perform His works before the people there (v. 3). Their remarks were made out of sarcasm, however, for the Bible says, "For not even His brothers were believing in Him" (v. 5). (Actually, these "brothers" were half-brothers, for Jesus was virgin born.)

Jesus told HIs brothers, "My time is not yet here" (v. 6). Similar statements are made in verses 8 and 30: "My time has not yet fully come"; "His hour had not yet come." It was evident that the Lord Jesus Christ was working on a divine timetable and that He did not choose to run ahead of schedule. The time would come when events would lead up to His betrayal and crucifixion, but He was not yet ready to allow those circumstances to come about.

At the Feast of Tabernacles
Jesus told His brothers to go to the feast, and He stayed in Galilee (vv. 8-9). However, after His brothers were gone Jesus also went to the feast, arriving in the middle of the week (v. 14). The Feast of Tabernacles lasted seven days, with a special holy day at the end of that time. There was much discussion about the Lord Jesus Christ even before He came, but "no one was speaking openly of Him for fear of the Jews" (v. 13). This reference indicates John's use of the word "Jews" to refer to the rulers of the Jews (see vv. 26, 48). Those who were afraid to speak openly were also Jews but it was because of their fear of the rulers that they did not make their opinions public.

On arriving in Jerusalem, Jesus went to the temple and began teaching. The Jewish leaders were amazed at the way He taught because they knew He had not been trained in their rabbinical schools. Yet his teaching made it apparent that He had superior knowledge.

Jesus told them that His doctrine did not originate with Himself but with the One who sent Him (v. 16). Referring to the Heavenly Father, He said, "If anyone is willing to do His will, he will know of the teaching, whether it is of God or whether I speak from Myself" (v. 17).

Inconsistent Legalism
The Jews before whom Jesus spoke prided themselves in keeping the Law, so He struck home to their hearts when He asked, "Did not Moses give you the Law, and yet none of you carries out the Law? Why do you seek to kill Me?" (v. 19). A common penalty for breaking the Law was death, so Christ was focusing attention on the fact that they deserved death if He did.

The Jewish leaders responded: "You have a demon! Who seeks to kill You?" (v. 20). One must understand that there is only one Devil, though there are many demons.

The people did not understand Jesus' charge that someone was trying to kill Him, for apparently no one was endeavoring to do so at the time. Jesus was probably referring to the incident recorded in John 5 that had taken place in Jerusalem earlier. He had healed a lame man on the Sabbath and, because of this, the Jews were persecuting Him (v. 16).

As Jesus talked to the Jewish rulers, He showed how inconsistent they really were. He pointed out that they carried out circumcision even if it fell on a Sabbath day and then said "If a man receives circumcision on the Sabbath so that the Law of Moses will not be broken, are you angry with Me because I made an entire man well on the Sabbath?" (7:23).

Doubts Concerning Jesus
As some of the Jews heard Jesus speak, they asked among themselves, "Is this not the man whom they are seeking to kill?" (v. 25). These people couldn't imagine that He would be speaking so boldly if His life was in danger. Yet they reasoned that He must not be the Christ, or Messiah, saying, "We know where this man is from; but whenever the Christ may come, no one knows where He is from" (v. 27). Many believed that the Messiah would mysteriously appear from nowhere, so they reasoned that Jesus was not the Messiah since they knew where He was from.

Jesus pointed out, however, that He had been sent by another "whom you do not know. I know Him, because I am from Him, and He sent Me" (vv. 28-29). It was apparent to the Jews that Jesus was again putting Himself on a level equal to God, so "they were seeking to seize Him; and no man laid his hand on Him, because His hour had not yet come" (v. 30). People were entirely helpless in capturing Jesus until He was willing to let Himself be taken by them.

Many people "believed in Him" (v. 31) because they reasoned that even the Messiah would not do more miracles than He. The Pharisees became so angry with the favorable response Jesus received from the people that they, along with the chief priests, "sent officers to seize Him" (v. 32).

Apparently these officers were to listen carefully to His speech in order to level some charge against Him. Their lack of success is seen later in this chapter.

Invitation to Thirsty Souls

On the last day of the feast, Jesus exclaimed, "If anyone is thirsty, let him come to Me and drink. He who believes in Me, as the Scripture said, 'From his innermost being will flow rivers of living water" (vv. 37-38). These statements are difficult to understand by themselves, but the next verse makes clear what Jesus meant: "But this He spoke of the Spirit, whom those who believed in Him were to receive; for the Spirit was not yet given, because Jesus was not yet glorified" (v. 39).

These events were taking place before Christ died on the cross and ascended to the Heavenly Father. The Holy Spirit did not come to take up residence in every believer until the Day of Pentecost, ten days after Christ ascended into heaven. These verses are a promise that anyone who believes in Jesus Christ as personal Savior will receive the Holy Spirit and that the characteristics of His life will flow out through the believer's life. The characteristics of the Holy Spirit are listed in Galatians 5:22-23, where they are referred to as "the fruit of the Spirit."

Hated by the Pharisees

Some of the Jews definitely thought Jesus was the Christ, but others still did not think so (John 7:43). Those who had animosity toward Him tried to take Him, but again were unable to do so (v. 44). The officers who had been sent by the Pharisees and chief priests then returned with this report: "Never has a man spoken the way this man speaks" (v. 46). They had been unable to level even a false charge against the Lord Jesus Christ. The Pharisees were so upset with these officers that they accused them of being deceived themselves (v. 47).

The Pharisees and chief priests had made up their minds

that here was no possibility of Jesus being the Messiah. As far as they were concerned, the case was closed. At this point, however, Nicodemus raised a significant question: "Our Law does not judge a man unless it first hears from him and knows what he is doing, does it?" (v. 51).

Although Nicodemus did not specifically defend Jesus, his comments amounted to a defense. The prejudice of the Jewish rulers was evident in what they said to him: "You are not also from Galilee, are you? Search, and see that no prophet arises out of Galilee" (v. 52). This statement was not technically correct inasmuch as Jonah and Nahum had come from Galilee, but the Pharisees and chief priests were so stirred up about Jesus that they were totally unconcerned about the facts. They were also ignorant of where Christ had been born. Their statements indicate they thought He was born in Galilee, instead of in Judea, the city of Bethlehem.

An Attempt to Trick Jesus

John 8:1-11 tells of a woman who had been caught in the act of adultery and had been brought to Jesus by the scribes and pharisees. They posed a question concerning her which they hoped would trap Him into condemning Himself. They reminded Jesus, "Now in the Law Moses commanded us to stone such women (v. 5). Then they asked Him, "What then do You say?" (v. 5). If He answered that she should be stoned, He would be in trouble with the Roman government because at the time only it had the authority to order capital punishment. On the other hand, if He said she should not be stoned, it would indicate He was unconcerned about the Mosaic Law and was therefore not qualified to be the Messiah.

In his wisdom Jesus answered nothing; instead, He bent over, and with His finger He wrote on the ground (v. 6). When they insisted on an answer, He said, "He who is without sin among you, let him be the first to throw a stone at her" (v. 7). Then He continued writing on the ground. One by one the accusers came under conviction and left until only the woman and Jesus remained. He then told her, "Go. From now on sin no more" (v. 11).

Not Without Another Witness

On another occasion, Jesus told the Pharisees, "I am the Light of the world; he who follows Me will not walk in the darkness, but will have the Light of life" (v. 12). Such a claim upset the Pharisees, so they responded by endeavoring to point out that Jesus was the only one who said this was so. Therefore, they did not need to give serious consideration to it. They were operating under the commonly accepted rule that everything should be confirmed by at least two witnesses (Matt. 18:16).

Jesus told the Pharisees that He was not alone in His witness because the Father had sent Him; thus, the Father was a witness also (John 8:18). The Pharisees then wanted to see His Father, but Jesus told them they did not know Him or His Father (v. 19). As the Apostle John wrote His Gospel, he pinpointed where Jesus spoke these words: "in the treasury, as he taught in the temple; and no one seized Him, because His hour had not yet come" (v. 20).

Jesus then began talking about going away and said those to whom He was speaking would not be able to come after Him (v. 21). These Jews did not understand what He was talking about, but He made clear why they were not able to follow Him: "You will die in your sins; for unless you believe that I am He, you will die in your sins" (v. 24). The Pharisees and chief priests had not understood what Jesus meant when He talked about going away (7:33-36), and neither did the Jews who heard Him in the temple (8:21-22).

The Eternal "I am"

Three verses in John 8 particularly emphasize the deity of Jesus Christ—that He Himself was, and is God. In each of these verses (vv. 24, 28, 58), Jesus used the expression "I am." Previously He had made such statements as "I am the Light of the world" (8:12), but in these three verses He simply says "I am" without adding anything further. In verses 24 and 28 the translators added the word "He," but the word is printed in italics, indicating that it was added by the translators. The word "He" does not appear in the original language—Christ said only "I am."

This is a direct reference to the way God revealed Himself to Moses at the burning bush. When God told Moses to return to the Israelites, Moses asked the Lord what he was to say when the people asked concerning God, "What is His name?" (Ex. 3:13). God told Moses to answer, "Thus you shall say to the sons of Israel, 'I AM has sent me to you" (v. 14).

In the words "I am" the timeless nature of God is revealed. He did not refer to the past or to the future but simply said "I am," indicating that He has always existed and will always exist.

The Jews whom Jesus was addressing as He spoke in the temple were well acquainted with the Old Testament expression "I am." This is why they became so angry—they recognized that Jesus was putting Himself on the level of God. Omit the unnecessary "He" and notice how Jesus drove home His point in John 8:24: "For unless you believe that I am . . . , you will die in your sins." Unless they recognized that He was God there was no hope of salvation for them.

Omitting the unnecessary "He" from verse 28 also adds emphasis to the deity of Christ. Jesus told the Jews: "When you lift up the Son of Man, then you will know that I am . . . , and I do nothing on My own initiative, but I speak these things as the Father taught Me."

Bondage, Not Freedom

The Bible says, "As He spoke these things, many came to believe in Him" (v. 30). Apparently they believed more information about Him but did not accept Him as Savior. This is indicated by what Jesus said to these people: "If you continue in My word, then you are truly disciples of Mine" (v. 31). That these people did not "believe" in a saving relationship is indicated later when they attempted to stone

Him for claiming to be greater than Abraham (vv. 58-59).

Their lack of belief in Him as Savior is also seen in that Jesus talked to them about freedom in Him, and yet they were not able to see that they needed any such freedom. He told them, "You will know the truth, and the truth will make you free" (v. 32). But they responded, "We are Abraham's descendants and have never yet been enslaved to anyone; how is it that You say, 'You will become free'?" (v. 33).

How strange that they made such a statement, for the nation of Israel had been in bondage to other nations during their history and were even then under the domination of the Roman Empire. But Christ revealed that He was talking about far more than just being under the domination of an earthly rulership. He said, "Everyone who commits sin is the slave of sin" (v. 34). The words "commits sin" actually mean "practices sin." Jesus was not referring to committing an individual act of sin; He was referring to living in sin as a way of life, which would indicate a person had never really trusted Him as Savior.

Spiritual Fatherhood

The dispute over freedom led to a discussion of origin. The Jews claimed that Abraham was their father (v. 39). Jesus pointed out that if they were truly the children of Abraham, their lives would evidence it. He was obviously referring to more than physical birth.

When the people claimed God as their Father, Jesus told them, "If God were your Father, you would love Me, for I proceeded forth and have come from God, for I have not even come on My own initiative, but He sent Me" (v. 42). Jesus then told them who their father was: "You are of your father the devil, and you want to do the desires of your father. He was a murderer from the beginning, and does not stand in the truth because there is no truth in him. Whenever he speaks a lie, he speaks from his own nature, for he is a liar and the father of lies" (v. 44).

God is the father of all in the broad sense because all

mankind has been created by God. But in a specific sense He is not the Father of unbelievers—the Devil is their father. When we hear people today referring to the "Fatherhood of God," it is important to distinguish what they really mean by such a statement. Do they mean only that God has created all mankind or do they mean that all are in a right relationship with God? Not everyone is in right relationship with God and, according to the words of Christ, the father of all unbelievers is the Devil.

Animosity of the Jewish Leaders

The Jews could not accept these statements by Christ, so they claimed He had a demon (v. 48). Jesus denied that and said, "if anyone keeps My word he will never see death" (v. 51). Then the Jews thought for sure He had a demon. They said, "Abraham died, and the prophets also; and You say, 'If anyone keeps My word, he will never taste of death.' Surely You are not greater than our father Abraham, who died? The prophets died too; whom do You make Yourself out to be? (vv. 52-53).

At this time Jesus spoke the third "I am" recorded in John 8: "Truly, truly, I say to you, before Abraham was born, I am" (v. 58). Such a bold claim to being equal with God upset these Jews: "Therefore they picked up stones to throw at Him, but Jesus hid Himself and went out of the temple" (v. 59).

Believing About Jesus Insufficient

From this chapter we see clearly that Jesus is God Himself and that anyone who has not trusted Him as personal Savior is spiritually dead and has no relationship with Jesus Christ. We also see from this chapter that it is not sufficient to have information about Jesus in order to have salvation, for some of the Jews "came to believe in Him" (v. 30), yet they later demonstrated that they had not trusted Him as Savior because they "picked up stones to throw at Him" (v. 59).

What is your relationship with Jesus Christ? Perhaps you know a great deal of information about Him, but have you personally trusted Him as your Savior? Have you recognized that only He has paid the penalty for your sin and is able to deliver you from condemnation?

Study Questions

1. What do the opening verses of John 7 reveal about Jesus' brothers? Perhaps you are from an unbelieving family, or you may know a Christian friend whose family does not believe. What difficulties do believers face among their unbelieving relatives?

---

2. How did some of the Jews in Jerusalem arrive at the conclusion that Jesus couldn't be the Messiah? What caused others to believe anyway? Even today two people may listen to the same gospel message and one may believe while the other turns away? How is this possible?

---

3. In John 8 the Jews tried to trap Jesus by asking HIs opinion about a woman who had been caught in the act of adultery. In the light of the Mosaic Law, Why was it inconsistent that only the woman was brought before Him? (see Lev. 20:10; Deut. 22:22).

_____

_____

_____

_____

_____

4. How did Jesus respond to the woman's accusers? Do you sometimes find yourself quick to judge someone else's sin? What will help you to be less judgmental?

_____

_____

_____

_____

_____

5. What is the significance of Jesus' use of the words "I am" in John 8:24, 28, 58 in referring to Himself?

_____

_____

_____

_____

_____

6. Explain how John 8:30 can say "many came to believe in Him" when later in the chapter these same people attempt to stone Christ. Have you ever met someone who believed certain facts about Jesus but had never believed in Him for salvation? What difficulties might you encounter in witnessing to such a person?

_____

_____

_____

_____

_____

_____

Chapter 6 – Physical and Spiritual Blindness

IS ALL SICKNESS A result of sin? Is there more than one kind of blindness? How do you witness to those who do not believe that Jesus Christ is God?

John 9 answers each of these questions. Although the chapter tells of incidents that happened in the first century, it reveals information that people desperately need today.

Physical Affliction
One day Jesus and his disciples passed a man who had been blind from his birth. The common understanding of the day was that any physical problem was directly related to a specific sin a person had committed. This reveals that the thinking of that day was not much different that the thinking today. Many people assume that if a person is sick it is because he has committed sin and God is judging him for it. But what do the Scriptures say?

The disciples asked Jesus, "Rabbi, who sinned, this man or his parents, that he would be born blind?" (v. 2). Their question revealed that the disciples held the common view of their day—that a physical handicap was the direct result of a specific sin.

Sometimes this is true. In writing to the Corinthians about misconduct at the Lord's table, Paul states, "For he who eats and drinks, eats and drinks judgment to himself if he does not judge the body rightly. For this reason many among you are weak and sick, and a number sleep" (1 Cor. 11:29-30). Some

Corinthian believers had physical ailments because of their sin at the Lord's table. Some had even experienced physical death, as indicated by the word "sleep," which was used in referring to a Christian's death.

Affliction Not Necessarily Punishment

Is physical suffering always the direct result of a specific sin? Jesus answered the question when He told His disciples: "It was neither that this man sinned, nor his parents; but it was so that the works of God might be displayed in him" (John 9:3). So we learn from this verse that physical problems are sometimes totally unrelated to a specific sin but are for the purpose of bringing glory to God.

This was the case with the "thorn in the flesh" (2 Cor. 12:7), which the Apostle Paul experienced. Paul asked the Lord on three different occasions to remove it from him, but the Lord told Paul, "My grace is sufficient for you, for power is perfected in weakness" (v. 9). So Paul said, "Most gladly, therefore, I will rather boast about my weaknesses, so that the power of Christ may dwell in me. Therefore I am well content with weaknesses, with insults, with distresses, with persecutions, with difficulties, for Christ's sake; for when I am weak, then I am strong (vv. 9-10).

It is important for the believer to recognize that any physical limitations he has are to be used to bring glory to God. This means one must recognize that God is sovereign and will supply the grace to endure any situation.

Spiritual Blindness

Concerning the man born blind, Christ told His disciples, "We must work the works of Him who sent Me as long as it is day; night is coming when no one can work. While I am in the world, I am the Light of the world" (John 9:4-5). In this setting involving a man who was physically blind, Christ talked about day and night and also about light, which was in contrast to darkness. Previously Jesus had said, "I am the Light of the world; he who follows Me will not walk in the darkness, but will have the Light of life" (8:12).

As the Lord spoke to His disciples concerning blindness, He had much more in mind than physical blindness, but He did not overlook the physical needs of the one before Him. After Jesus had spoken to His disciples, "He spat on the ground, and made clay of the spittle, and applied the clay to his eyes" (9:6).

The Use of Means
Note that Jesus used a means, or a process, to heal this man's blindness. As the Son of God it was certainly not necessary for Him to use any means at all; He was able to bring instantaneous healing. Not only did Jesus heal all kinds of diseases instantaneously, but in particular He healed blindness in this way.

The gospel of Matthew records several instances where Jesus healed the blind, and there is no mention of means being used (9:29-30; 12:22; 15:30; 21:14). The account in Matthew 9 concerning the two blind men says, "Then He touched their eyes, saying, It shall be done to you according to your faith." And their eyes were opened" (vv. 29-30). This seemed to be the normal way Christ dealt with blindness. Why then did He use a process when He healed the blind man mentioned in John 9?

The Scriptures do not specifically say why Jesus used a process in the healing recorded in John 9. Not only did Jesus make clay and put it on the eyes of this blind man, but He also told him: "Go, wash in the pool of Siloam" (which is translated, Sent)" (v. 7). Even though we do not know why Jesus used this particular process, it reveals to us that sometimes God chooses to use various means to bring about healing.

Some today consider healing to be only that which is instantaneous, not involving any process at all. However, John

9 reveals this is not always the case. In fact although God is able to heal anyone instantaneously, this does not seem to be His normal manner of working today.

God Not Obligated to Heal

It is especially important to realize that God is not obligated to heal a believer. In fact, the physical limitation itself is sometimes used to bring glory to God in a way that would not be possible if the limitation did not exist (see 2 Cor. 12:7-10). Sometimes God uses the medical profession in helping to eliminate disease—remember, Luke was a physician (see Col. 4:14). It is also interesting to note in the Scriptures that even though the apostles, as direct representatives of the Lord Jesus Christ, had the ability to heal others, they did not always do so. The Apostle Paul specifically mentioned leaving Trophimus sick at Miletus (2 Tim. 4:20).

A Miracle

After Jesus told the blind man to go wash in the pool of Siloam, "he went away and washed, and came back seeing" (John 9:7). Imagine what a stir this caused! It was common knowledge that this person had been born blind, yet now he was able to see. How to explain this was a tremendous problem both to his neighbors and to the religious leaders of his day.

Some of the neighbors thought it was the same blind person they had known before who made it a practice to sit and beg (v. 8). Others, however, decided this person looked like that one but must not be the same but he told them, "I am the one" (v. 9).

When the neighbors asked the man to explain how he was now able to see he rehearsed what Jesus had done for him. Notice that he referred to Jesus by the words "The man who is called Jesus" (v. 11). The man knew how others referred to this Person who had healed him, but he knew little else about Jesus, as is evident from the rest of the chapter.

Quibbling, Questioning Pharisees
When the neighbors asked the man where the One who had healed him now was, he answered, "I do not know" (v. 12). The neighbors then brought the man to the Pharisees. When the Pharisees learned that this healing had taken place on the Sabbath Day (v. 14), they were more concerned about Jesus having broken the Sabbath than they were about the blind man being healed.

To some of the Pharisees it was obvious that Jesus was definitely not of God because He broke the Sabbath; however, others could not understand how He had the ability to heal blindness if He was not of God. (v. 16). Not being able to agree on this matter, they then decided to question whether the man really had been blind. The religious leaders refused to believe he had actually been blind until they heard what his parents had to say.

When the man's parents were called before the Pharisees and asked about their son's condition, they said, "We know that this is our son, and that he was born blind; but how he now sees, we do not know; or who opened his eyes, we do not know. Ask him; he is of age, he will speak for himself" (vv. 20-21). The following verse reveals why these parents answered as they did: "They were afraid of the Jews; for the Jews had already agreed that if anyone confessed Him to be Christ, he was to be put out of the synagogue" (v. 22). This shows the animosity that the Jews had toward Jesus and toward anyone who followed Him. Because the parents feared excommunication, they refused to take a position concerning Jesus and left their son to defend himself.

The Man's Testimony
Since the Jews did not receive their answer from the parents, they again began to interrogate the man who had been healed. However, the Jews really weren't serious in wanting to learn information about Jesus; they had already decided that He was guilty. This is evident from what the Jews said concerning Jesus: "We know that this man is a sinner" (v. 24). But note

the beautiful testimony of the man born blind: "Whether He is a sinner, I do not know; one thing I do know, that though I was blind, now I see" (v. 25).

This man was willing to let the Jews hassle over the theological problems concerning Jesus, but no one could rob him of the fact that he knew experientially that he had been born blind but now was able to see. The man did not seek to defend Jesus; he simply gave the facts and let them speak for themselves.

Cross-Examination

Because the Jews were so frustrated, they again asked what Jesus did to this man. Imagine the pressure this man was under! He was standing before the most highly educated people in Israel who were accustomed to being honored by all Jews for their lofty position as defenders of the Mosaic Law. This man was totally unaccustomed to such an audience; having been born blind, he was uneducated and had spent his life as a beggar.

But as the Jews cross-examined this man, he not only answered them with boldness but also put them on the spot. He asked why they wanted to hear the report again—did they want to become Jesus' disciples? (v. 27). This really upset the Jews, and they said, "You are His disciple, but we are disciples of Moses (v.28). This verse shows the sharp distinction that had been drawn between the followers of Moses and the followers of Jesus. Although Jesus was the prophet Moses said would come, those defending the Mosaic Law rejected the very one Moses spoke of.

When the Pharisees admitted they did not know the origin of Jesus, the healed blind man again took the offensive and attacked their competency. He said to them: "Well, here is an amazing thing, that you do not know where He is from, and yet He opened my eyes. . . . Since the beginning of time it has never been heard that anyone opened the eyes of a person born blind. If this man were not from God, He could do nothing. (vv. 30, 32-33). The learned Jews were not about to be instructed and put on the spot by this uneducated beggar, so they threw him out of their midst (v. 34).

Healed Man Unsaved

When Jesus heard that this man had been thrown out by the Jews, He found him and asked, "Do you believe in the Son of Man?" (v. 35). The man who had been healed then answered, "Who is He, Lord, that I may believe in Him?" (v. 36). This question revealed that the man did not know Jesus Christ as Savior at the time he was healed.

This contrasts with some modern-day "healers" who work only with believers and maintain that the afflicted believer must have enough faith to be healed. But this man whom Christ healed wasn't even a Christian; all he really knew about Jesus at the time he was healed was His name (v.11).

The Purpose of Miracles

The special miracles that Jesus and His direct representatives, the apostles, performed were to show that Jesus was truly the Messiah and to confirm the message He gave through the apostles. It is interesting to notice the use of the words "signs, wonders, and miracles," as the Bible refers to them. On the Day of Pentecost, when Peter addressed the Israelites, he said concerning Jesus, "Men of Israel, listen to these words: Jesus the Nazarene, a man attested to you by God with miracles and wonders and signs which God performed through Him in your midst, just as you yourselves know" (Acts 2:22). In this verse we see that miracles, wonders and signs were performed by Jesus in order to show He was approved by God.

That the apostles, as direct representatives of Jesus Christ, also had the ability to perform signs, wonders, and miracles is evident from what Paul told the Corinthians: "The signs of a true apostle were performed among you with all perseverance, by signs and wonders and miracles" (2 Cor. 12:12).

The Message Confirmed

The message of salvation, as proclaimed by Jesus and HIs

special representatives, was also confirmed by signs, wonders, and miracles. Hebrews 2:3,4 says, "How will we escape if we neglect so great a salvation? After it was at the first spoken through the Lord, it was confirmed to us by those who heard, God also testifying with them, both by signs and wonders and by various miracles and by gifts of the Holy Spirit according to His own will?"

It is important to realize that when something has been confirmed, there is no need to keep on confirming it. The Book of Hebrews was written shortly before the destruction of Jerusalem in A.D. 70, and at this time the writer viewed the message as having been confirmed (by miracles, signs, and wonders) in the past (v. 3). There was no indication that the confirming was still going on at the time he wrote.

Inasmuch as signs, wonders and miracles confirmed Jesus Christ as the Messiah, the apostles as His special representatives, and the message as being from God, there is no need for the confirming signs to exist any longer. Now the question is whether or not a person will believe what has been confirmed. If a person will not believe in the message of the Bible, which God has confirmed, God is not obligated in any way to provide a special sign for that person.

Healed Man Converted
The healing of the blind man, recorded in John 9, was another miracle Jesus performed to confirm the fact that He was of God and was qualified to be the Messiah. The fact that this miracle was performed on an unbeliever was especially significant. If a person claiming to be the Messiah could perform miracles only on those who already believed in Him, this would be highly suspicious. But if He could perform a miracle like this on one who did not know anything about Him, this would be extremely impressive to an unbelieving world.

After Jesus Christ explained to the man who He was, the man responded: "Lord, I believe. And he worshiped Him" (v. 38). This was the moment of salvation for the man who had been born blind. By an act of his will he trusted Jesus Christ and what He could do for him. When that transfer of trust took place, the man came into possession of eternal life and was delivered from condemnation.

Spiritual Blindness
Having healed this man who was once physically blind, Jesus said, "For judgment I came into this world, so that those who do not see may see, and that those who see may become blind" (v. 39). Here, Jesus was using the parallel of physical sight to refer to spiritual sight. This man had received his physical sight, but more importantly he had received spiritual sight. However, those who think they already see without having made a decision for Jesus Christ will have their spiritual blindness revealed when the Savior appears.

The Pharisees who were listening in on Jesus' conversation with the man realized that Jesus might be referring to them, so they asked: "We are not blind too, are we?" (v. 40). Jesus answered: "If you were blind, you would have no sin; but since you say, 'We see,' your sin remains" (v. 41). Here again Jesus was using the parallel of physical sight to teach truths concerning spiritual sight. Because the Pharisees claimed to have spiritual sight and yet rejected Jesus as the Messiah, He told them, "Your sin remains" (v. 41). The Pharisees had witnessed sufficient evidence to realize that Jesus was sent from God, but they had willfully rejected Him, so they remained in their sins.

How tragic it was that these who actually had the privilege of seeing Jesus Christ personally rejected Him as Savior. But it is just as tragic for those today who have heard the way of salvation and have refused to trust Jesus Christ as personal Savior. Have you made this decision? If not, do so before it is eternally too late!

Study Questions
1. As was true in Jesus' day, many people today still believe that illness and suffering are a direct result of an

individual's sin. Citing Jesus' teaching in John 9, explain why this view is not necessarily true. What other scriptural examples relate to this issue?

_____

_____

_____

_____

_____

2. After the blind man in John was healed, why was there so much debate about whether he was really born blind? Why were his parents reluctant to defend him? Have you ever found yourself reluctant to defend a friend when his faith was being challenged? What causes this reluctance? What can you do to overcome it?

_____

_____

_____

_____

_____

3. What was the purpose of the miracles that Jesus and His apostles performed? What is your response to reports of miracles, signs, and wonders in today's world?

_____

_____

_____

_____

_____

4. Some teachers today insist that physical healing is dependent on the person's having sufficient faith. How does the experience of the blind man refute this claim?

_____

_____

_____

_____

5. What parallel did Jesus draw between physical blindness and spiritual blindness? What is the cure for spiritual blindness?

_____

_____

_____

_____

_____

_____

_____

_____

_____

_____

_____

_____

_____

_____

_____

Chapter 7 – Jesus, the Shepherd and Life-Giver

THE BLIND MAN WHO had heard the voice of Jesus and had then responded for healing was expelled by the Jews. Jesus found the man and led him to salvation. This provided the setting for what Jesus told the Jews, as recorded in John 10.

Jesus told the questioning Pharisees, "Truly, truly, I say to you, he who does not enter by the door into the fold of the sheep, but climbs up some other way, he is a thief and a robber. But he who enters by the door is a shepherd of the sheep. To him the doorkeeper opens, and the sheep hear his voice, and he calls his own sheep by name and leads them out" (vv. 1-3).

The Sheepfold

In these statements Jesus was using the analogy of the sheepfold, with which the Pharisees would have been well acquainted. It was common for one sheepfold to contain sheep belonging to several shepherds. In the morning, a shepherd would come to the fold and be admitted by the porter, or doorkeeper, and when the shepherd gave his unique call, only his own sheep would follow him.

Jesus emphasized that the sheep know the voice of the shepherd and they will not follow a stranger (vv. 4-5). This emphasis was no doubt for the purpose of stressing that the blind man had heard His voice and had followed Him instead of following them.

The "fold of the sheep" (v. 1) is a reference to Judaism, as is indicated by Jesus' reference to other sheep (Gentiles) which were not of this fold (v. 16). Jesus emphasized to the Pharisees that He had legitimate access to the sheepfold of Judaism. Not only had Old Testament prophecy told of His coming, but He had also performed miracles which proved He was sent from God. Therefore, He was qualified to enter the fold, although not all responded to His voice. The blind man had responded, and others had believed in Him as Savior, but many had not responded, which proved they were not really His sheep.

The Shepherd and His Sheep

When Jesu had finished this story, the Pharisees did not understand what he was trying to tell them (v. 6). Jesus further explained by drawing an analogy to the relationship of the shepherd and his sheep during the daytime. In the first part of John 10 Jesus described the shepherd's coming to the fold in the morning for the sheep. Then He told of the shepherd's care for the sheep during the day. When Jesus said, 'I am the door of the sheep" (v. 7), He was not referring to the sheepfold (v. 1) of Judaism. He had entered the sheepfold as a shepherd and had called His sheep to Him; now He was explaining His relationship to His own sheep.

Concerning the door mentioned in verse 7, one competent Bible expositor has said, "We must understand the door as representing the entrance perhaps to a wooded thicket where a sheep would enter to find shade and water and from which it would pass to find pasturage" (*Light in the Darkness,* p. 140). This statement agrees with the context, for Jesus said, "I am the door; if anyone enters through Me, he will be saved, and will go in and out and find pasture" (v. 9).

Sometimes a shepherd and his sheep would be so far from the sheepfold at night that they would have to remain out in the open. This was dangerous because of the threat of thieves and wild animals. However, Jesus emphasized that He had come not only so His sheep could have life but also so they could have abundant life (v. 10). As the Good Shepherd, He was willing to lay down His life for His sheep, whereas a hired hand would run away to save his own life and let the sheep be scattered or killed by the wolves. Jesus' mention of the hired hand (vv. 12-13), seems to be a clear reference to the Pharisees, who were concerned about their professions but were really not concerned about the people they served.

One Flock and One Shepherd
Jesus explained, "I have other sheep, which are not of this fold; I must bring them also, and they will hear My voice; and they will become one flock with one shepherd" (v. 16). A contrast is seen in this verse by the different Greek words used for "fold" and "flock." The one used in referring to "this fold" is different than the word used when Jesus said there shall be "one flock."

The first "fold" is a reference to those in Judaism who had responded to Jesus' voice. Thus, the other sheep would be Gentiles, and together the saved Jews and Gentiles would comprise "one flock." And this flock would have "one shepherd." Jesus was here referring to the universal Church, also known as His body, which is comprised of every person who has received Him as Savior during this age. The Body of Christ is referred to in 1 Corinthians 12:13: "For by one Spirit we were all baptized into one body, whether Jews or Greeks, whether slaves or free, and we were all made to drink of one Spirit."

Jesus' talk about the one flock and one shepherd, as well as His ability to lay down His life and to take it up again (John 10:17-18), caused a division among the Jews (v. 19). Some thought He had a demon and was mad (v. 20), but others could not understand how it was possible for a demon to open the eyes of the blind (v. 21). (This reference to the blind shows that the healing of the blind man [John 9] provided the direct background for the comments recorded in John 10.)

The Believer's Position in Christ

As the Apostle John wrote his Gospel, he next referred to the Feast of Dedication (Hanukkah), which took place during the wintertime at Jerusalem (v. 22). The Jews gathered around Jesus and urged Him to specifically tell them whether or not He was the Christ (Messiah) (v. 24). Jesus replied: "I told you, and you do not believe; the works that I do in My Father's name, these testify of Me. But you do not believe because you are not of My sheep" (vv. 25-26). Here again Jesus alluded to sheep and to the fact that they respond to the voice of their own shepherd.

Jesus then made some of the most direct comments recorded in the Scriptures concerning the position of believers in Christ: "My sheep hear My voice, and I know them, and they follow Me; and I give eternal life to them, and they will never perish; and no one will snatch them out of My hand. My Father, who has given them to Me, is greater than all; and no one is able to snatch them out of the Father's hand" (vv. 27-29). These statements clearly reveal that when a person trusts Jesus Christ as his Savior, he is secure in Christ—no one is able to pluck him out of the hand of Christ or out of the hand of the Father.

Angry Disbelievers

Jesus emphasized again His oneness with the Father when He said, "I and the Father are one" (v. 30). This angered the Jews so much that they began to pick up stones in order to stone Him to death for blasphemy (vv. 31, 33).

Jesus told the Jews, "If I do not do the works of My Father, do not believe Me; but if I do them, though you do not believe Me, believe the works, so that you may know and understand that the Father is in Me, and I in the Father" (vv. 37-38). The Jews were again angered by this kind of talk and tried to capture Him, "and He eluded their grasp" (v. 39).

After this encounter with the Pharisees in Jerusalem, Jesus went away to the other (east) side of the Jordan River. Even there many recognized Him (vv. 40-41), and "many believed in Him there" (v. 42).

The Raising of Lazarus

As the Apostle John told of some of the things Jesus did that proved He was God, he told of the raising of a dead man. This was the seventh miracle he specifically mentioned. The account centered around three people who lived in Bethany— Lazarus, Mary and Martha (11:1). It is evident from this story that Jesus was especially fond of these three. When Lazarus became ill, his sisters sent for Jesus because they had confidence He could heal Lazarus (v. 3). But even after Jesus heard the news that Lazarus was sick, He stayed where He was two more days before He started for Judea (vv. 6-7).

Purposeful Delay

To Mary and Martha, this must have seemed like an excessively long delay. Why didn't Jesus start for Bethany as soon as He heard the news about Lazarus' illness? The intent of Jesus was to teach Mary and Martha a spiritual lesson—one they would not have had impressed upon them as deeply if He would have arrived in Bethany sooner.

If the Lord Jesus Christ worked this way then, He can certainly work in a similar way today. He never changes—He is the same in the past, present and future (Heb. 13:8). Perhaps you are presently going through some extremely difficult time, and you wonder why God doesn't move to solve your problems. Of course, He could do so if He chose, so the fact that He has not moved yet reveals He has something more for you to learn. This is hard to appreciate at the time of difficulty—Mary and Martha probably had trouble appreciating it also. But when the Lord chose to come and act in their behalf, it is likely they would not have wanted it any other way—they learned to trust Jesus more because of His delay.

On to Bethany

When Jesus finally started His trip to Bethany, His disciples were worried about the way He was risking His life. Not too long ago the Jews had tried to kill Him, and now He was going back into this same area (v. 8). Jesus did not fear, however, because He knew He was serving the will of His Father, and no one could do anything to Him until the proper hour came.

Jesus told the disciples, "Our friend Lazarus has fallen asleep; but I go, so that I may awaken him out of sleep" (v. 11). The disciples saw no real problem if Lazarus was only sleeping, because he would wake out of his sleep, but Jesus made clear to them that He was referring to the fact that Lazarus had died (vv. 12-13). The word "sleep" is used elsewhere in the Scriptures to refer to believers who have died (1 Corinthians 15:6,51; 1 Thess. 4:13-15). It refers only to the body sleeping, never to the soul.

Reassuring Words

When Jesus arrived in Bethany, Lazarus had been dead for four days (John 11:17). Many Jews had gathered at the home to comfort Martha and Mary. When Martha learned that Jesus was coming, she went to meet Him and said, "Lord, if You had been here, my brother would not have died. Even now I know that whatever You ask of God, God will give You" (vv. 21-22). Jesus assured her that Lazarus would be raised again (v. 23), but Martha thought He was referring to the resurrection at the last day (v. 24). Jesus told her, "I am the resurrection and the life; he who believes in Me will live even if he dies, and everyone who lives and believes in Me will never die. Do you believe this?" (vv. 25-26).

The Compassionate Savior

Martha believed in the words of Jesus and went to get Mary, who quickly came to Jesus and fell at his feet saying, "Lord, if

You had been here, my brother would not have died" (v. 32). Jesus was deeply moved by the weeping of Mary and the Jews, and "He was deeply moved in spirit and was troubled" (v. 33). He asked where the body of Lazarus had been laid, and the degree of Jesus' concern is seen in the words "Jesus wept" (v. 35). This incident reveals that Jesus understands how a person feels at the time of the death of a loved one. "For we do not have a high priest who cannot sympathize with our weaknesses" (Heb. 4:15).

Mourners Who Lost Hope
Even the Jews who were gathered with Mary and Martha thought that surely this One who had the power to open the eyes of the blind could have prevented Lazarus from dying (John 11:37). But they were to witness an even greater miracle.

As Jesus came to the cave where the body of Lazarus had been placed, He said, "Remove the stone" (v. 39). Martha immediately responded, "Lord, by this time there will be a stench, for he has been dead four days" (v. 39). Martha did not want the stone removed. Since Lazarus had been dead four days, his body would be decomposing, and there would be an awful stench. In spite of the fact that Martha was standing in the presence of Jesus, who is the basis of hope, she had no hope concerning Lazarus.

For the Glory of God
Jesus told Martha, "Did I not say to you that if you believe, you will see the glory of God?" (v. 40). Jesus' purpose in this entire incident was to reveal the glory of God. In fact, Jesus indicated this purpose when He first heard that Lazarus was sick, saying, "This sickness is not to end in death, but for the glory of God, so that the Son of God may be glorified by it" (v. 4).

Jesus' desire was to always glorify the Father. After recording the miracle which occurred at the wedding feast, John wrote: "This beginning of His signs Jesus did in Cana of

Galilee, and manifested His glory" (2:11). As the glory of Jesus was revealed, the glory of the Father was also revealed.

Believers today should have the same desire—to glorify God in everything they do. Jesus told His followers, "Let your light shine before men in such a way that they may see your good works, and glorify your Father who is in heaven" (Matt. 5:16). Believers should have the same desire the Apostle Paul had: "According to my earnest expectation and hope, that I will not be put to shame in anything, but that with all boldness, Christ will even now, as always, be exalted in my body, whether by life or by death" (Phil 1:20).

The Lord of Life
Jesus came to Lazarus' grave and asked that the stone covering the entrance be taken away. After thanking the Heavenly Father for hearing His prayer, Jesus said, "Lazarus, come forth" (John 11:43). Lazarus came forth, "bound hand and foot with wrappings, and his face was wrapped around with a cloth. Jesus said to them, "Unbind him, and let him go" (v. 44).

Many who saw this miracle believed in Jesus Christ (v. 45). They needed no more evidence to convince them.

Stubborn Disbelief
One might think that after a tremendous miracle such as this, everyone would believe in Jesus Christ as personal Savior, but this was not so. A rich man wanted someone to rise from the dead and witness to his family. He was told, "If they do not listen to Moses and the Prophets, they will not be persuaded even if someone rises from the dead" (Luke 16:31).

This was precisely the case with the Pharisees after Lazarus had been raised from the dead—they still refused to believe in Jesus Christ. In fact, their hatred was more bitter than ever. A council of the chief priests and Pharisees was called, and this question was asked: "What are we doing? For this man is performing many signs. If we let Him go on like this, all men will believe in Him, and the Romans will come and take away both our place and our nation" (John 11:47-48).

This was a meeting of the Sanhedrin, the highest ruling body in Israel. They were extremely concerned over the prominence that Jesus was having in the nation. They were afraid that the Roman government would see the people in turmoil and take away the few remaining privileges they had.

A Prophetic Suggestion

The high priest suggested that there was no need for the whole nation to perish; instead it was necessary for only one person to die (v. 50). He was referring to the fact that if Jesus could be put to death there would be no need for the Roman Empire to intervene in Jewish affairs.

At this point, the Apostle John noted that these words of Caiaphas were really a prophecy of what would take place in God's program in order to provide salvation for all (vv. 51-52). Caiaphas and the others were unaware of the part they would have in fulfilling prophecy; from that time on they sought to put Jesus to death.

Jesus' Life in Danger

Apparently Jesus knew of the decision the Sanhedrin had made concerning Him, for the Bible says, "Therefore Jesus no longer continued to walk publicly among the Jews, but went away from there to the country near the wilderness, into a city called Ephraim; and there He stayed with the disciples" (v. 54).

Verses 55-57 tell of the Jewish Passover that was near and of the discussion among the people as to whether Jesus would show up for the Passover. Just in case He might "the chief priests and the Pharisees had given orders that if anyone knew where He was, he was to report it, so that they might seize Him" (v. 57).

It is hard to imagine the bitter animosity the chief priests and Pharisees had toward Jesus, yet many others had received Him as their Messiah. Those who did received forgiveness of sin and eternal life.

Study Questions

1. From Jesus' statements about "one flock with one shepherd" (John 10:16), what can you conclude about other Christians who may not belong to your particular church or denomination? Do you find it easy or difficult to fellowship with Christians outside your own group? Why? What do you think is God's ideal in such relationships?

_____

_____

_____

_____

_____

2. Read John 10:27-29. Do you worry that someday you may do something to cause you to lose your salvation? How does this passage relate to such concerns?

_____

_____

_____

_____

_____

3. Read the account of Lazarus' illness and death in John 11. How would you feel if you took a dear friend or family member to an emergency room and then no one bothered with him or her for several days? How would you feel if the patient died because the help you requested was delayed? Why did Jesus delay in responding to Mary and Martha's summons?

_____

_____

_____

_____

_____

4. What does the fact that Jesus was risking His life in going to Bethany say about His love for Lazarus and his sisters? Have you ever withheld your support or encouragement or even physical presence from someone who needed it because you feared what someone else might say? How did you feel about it later? If you faced the same situation today, how would you respond? Why?

_____

_____

_____

_____

5. The rich man was told in Luke 16:31 that even if one rose from the dead, people still would not believe God's truth. How was this statement supported by the raising of Lazarus?

Chapter 8 – Jesus' Death Appointed

JOHN 11 REVEALS THE close relationship Jesus had with Mary, Martha and Lazarus. This is also seen in chapter 12, for He ate a meal with them six days before Passover.

From the other Gospel writers we learn that the meal in Bethany took place in the house of Simon the leper (Matt. 26:6; Mark 14:3). Several persons attended this meal, but John focused his attention on Mary, Martha, and Lazarus. Martha helped with serving the meal, while Lazarus was reclining at the table with other guests at the table with Jesus (v. 2).

Mary's Love Offering
The attention of the entire group was fixed on Mary because of something highly unusual that she did. She poured some costly perfume on Jesus' feet and then wiped His feet with her hair (v. 3). Imagine the fragrance of the perfume that filled the house!

Complaining Judas
But Mary's act of devotion did not go unchallenged. Judas particularly spoke up concerning what she had done. Since "Judas" was a common name of that time, it was necessary for a writer to specify which Judas. The Apostle John did this in his Gospel when he said, "But Judas Iscariot, one of His disciples, who was intending to betray Him" (v. 4). John was writing these words near the close of the first century, after

these events had taken place; therefore, he was able to tell the reader at this point who it was that betrayed Jesus.

Judas asked, "Why was this perfume not sold for three hundred denarii and given to poor people?" (v. 5). The extent of Mary's sacrifice is indicated by what Judas thought it could be sold for—"three hundred denarii." The word translated "denarii" is the plural form of *dēnarion*, which referred to a Roman silver coin that was an average working man's wage in that day. The parable recorded in Matthew 20:1-16 reveals that a "*dēnarius*" was the wage for a day's labor (v. 2).

So the ointment, or perfume, with which Mary was anointing Jesus amounted to about a year's wages for a laboring man. What a deep devotion she had for the Savior!

Critical Disciples

More than just Judas grumbled at Mary because of this supposed waste. Matthew 26:8 indicates all the disciples complained about it. The fact that John singled out Judas indicates that Judas may have been the chief spokesman in the complaint.

John added concerning Judas, "Now he said this, not because he was concerned about the poor, but because he was a thief, and as he had the money box, he used to pilfer what was put into it" (John 12:6). The hypocrisy of Judas knew no end. By his statements he even implied that he knew better than Jesus did how the ointment should be used. And how noble it must have sounded for Judas to speak out for the poor! Surely no one would suspect his intentions to steal the money.

Jesus quickly cut off criticism concerning Mary by saying, "Let her alone, so that she may keep it for the day of My burial. For you always have the poor with you, but you do not always have Me" (vv. 7-8). From these words of Jesus it is clear that Mary understood He was going to die, a fact which the other disciples had difficulty in grasping. Jesus indicated that they would always have opportunity to help poor people but that He would not be with them physically forever.

Conspiring Religious Leaders
News got around that Jesus was at this particular house, and people began to gather not only to see Him but also to see Lazarus (v. 9). The fact that Lazarus had been raised from the dead caused him to be the center of attention along with Jesus. The presence of Lazarus was an embarrassment to the chief priests because he so clearly represented a miracle that Jesus had performed. Consequently, they made plans to kill Lazarus as well as Jesus (v. 10). This reveals the way unbelievers reason: Because they reject Jesus Christ as Savior, they also try to eliminate anything that reminds them of Him.

Jesus Rides Into Jerusalem
The next day Jesus went from Bethany to Jerusalem, where the Feast of the Passover was to be held. Many people from various places in that part of the world came to Jerusalem to observe the Passover and a crowd saw Jesus coming. They "took the branches of the palm trees and went out to meet Him, and began to shout, "Hosanna! BLESSED IS HE WHO COMES IN THE NAME OF THE LORD, even the King of Israel" (v. 13).

The Jews were then living under the oppression of the Roman Empire. They looked forward to the day when they would have a king who would throw off the yoke of Rome. Many hoped that Jesus would be that king, so as Jesus was headed for Jerusalem riding on a young donkey, they gave great honor to Him.

John referred to Zechariah 9:9 when he said that the events on that day were a fulfillment of what had been written (John 12:14-15). Jesus' disciples, however, did not realize the significance of what was taking place on that day. They did not fully understand the significance until after Jesus had risen from the dead (v. 16).

Part of the people's attraction to Jesus at this time was due to His having raised Lazarus from the dead. The people wanted to see the One who had performed this miracle (vv. 17-18). The Pharisees were completely frustrated as they saw the people flock toward Jesus because of this miracle. In disgust they blamed each other for being such failures that everyone was going after Jesus (v. 19).

Gentiles Seek Jesus
Among those who were coming to Jerusalem for the Feast of Passover were some Greeks who especially wanted to see Jesus. They first approached Philip, who went to tell Andrew. Then both Philip and Andrew approached Jesus with the request (vv. 21-22).

Jesus' answer was neither a direct yes or no concerning seeing these Greeks, but it amounted to yes—everyone would soon see Him because of His death, This request by the Greeks was significant because it indicated that more than just the Jews were concerned about Jesus.

Jesus' Hour Now Come
Inasmuch as Jesus had come to provide salvation for both Jew and Gentile, He answered, "The hour has come for the Son of Man to be glorified" (v. 23).

Notice the significant words "The hour has come." Earlier Jesus had said, "My hour has not yet come" (2:4). John had recorded that although the Jews were trying to kill Jesus, they could not lay hands on Him "because his hour had not yet come" (7:30). In the next chapter John said that as Jesus taught in the temple no one could lay hands on him "for his hour was not yet come" (8:20). But now Jesus said "The hour has come for the Son of Man to be glorified" (12:23). These words set in motion the last events of the earthly life of Jesus as He prepared to go to the cross and shed His blood for the sins of the world.

Having announced that His hour had come, Jesus said "Unless a grain of wheat falls into the earth and dies, it remains alone; but if it dies, it bears much fruit" (v. 24). In order for those who believe to receive eternal life and be delivered from condemnation, it was necessary for Christ to die on the cross.

Loving Life and Losing It
In addition to His analogy about the grain of wheat, Jesus said, "He who loves his life loses it, and he who hates his life in this world will keep it to life eternal" (v. 25).

Spiritual blessing has come on all mankind because Jesus willingly gave His life for others. The Apostle Paul told believers they should think in the same way the Lord Jesus Christ did: "Have this attitude in yourselves which was also in Christ Jesus, who, although He existed in the form of God, did not regard equality with God a thing to be grasped, but emptied Himself, taking the form of a bond-servant, and being made in the likeness of men. Being found in appearance as a man, He humbled Himself by becoming obedient to the point of death, even death on a cross" (Phil. 2:5-8).

The person who loves his life and seeks to satisfy himself at all costs will lose his life. This principle is true not only at the time of salvation but also in the Christian life. At the time of salvation, a person must be willing to give up all pride and confidence in anything else and place his trust in Jesus Christ alone as his Savior. Those not willing to give up all trust in other so-called means of salvation are not delivered from condemnation; thus, they love their lives but eventually lose them spiritually.

In the Christian life it is also important to put one's own desires aside and serve Jesus Christ only. Some believers are afraid that if they really give Him first place in their lives, He will require them to do something they do not want to do, But those who hold on to their lives in this way will never have complete fulfillment.

Jesus' Brief Prayer
Jesus then spoke to His heavenly Father and said, "Now My soul has become troubled; and what shall I say, 'Father, save Me from this hour'? But for this purpose I came to this hour" (John 12:27). On the surface, it seems that Christ was asking the Father even at this point to spare Him from the crucifixion. However, some Greek manuscripts have a

question mark after the word "hour." This would cause the verse to read: "What shall I say? Father, save me from this hour? But for this cause came I unto this hour."

Used in this way, Jesus would not have been asking to be spared form the hour of death but would have been focusing attention on the fact that the hour had finally come when He would give His life for the sin of the world. This was the primary purpose for His coming into the world, and finally the hour had come when His purpose would be culminated.

After Jesus told the Father: "Glorify Your name" (v. 28), a voice came from heaven saying, "I have both glorified it, and will glorify it again." Some of the people who heard the voice thought it had thundered; others thought an angel had spoken to Him. Jesus told those who heard the voice: "This voice has not come for My sake, but for your sakes" (v. 30). Jesus had no doubts about His part in the program of redemption, but those with Him at this time needed a confirmation that these things were of God.

Jesus viewed His hour as the time when judgment would come on the world and when the ruler of the world would be thrown out (v. 31). Hebrews 2:14 also refers to this same judgment: "Therefore, since the children share in flesh and blood, He Himself likewise also partook of the same, that through death He might render powerless him who had the power of death, that is, the devil." By His death, Jesus broke the power of Satan over all who will trust Him as Savior.

How Jesus Would Die

Jesus then indicated what kind of death He would die when He said, "And I, if I am lifted up from the earth, will draw all men to Myself" (John 12:32). John specifically stated that these remarks indicated "the kind of death by which He was to die" (v. 33). Earlier, Jesus had made a similar statement to Nicodemus: "As Moses lifted up the serpent in the wilderness, even so must the Son of Man be lifted up" (3:14).

In the crucifixion Jesus was lifted up above the earth and became the focal point of the attention of mankind. From this time on the decision that each person must make is, Will I believe in Jesus Christ and what He accomplished for me on the cross or not?

Blind Unbelief

Those who heard Jesus speak did not understand why He was talking about death, They had been looking for a king, and anyone realizes that a dead king is no king at all. However, Jesus told the people, "While you have the Light, believe in the Light, so that you may become sons of Light" (v. 36). He urged them to believe on Him while there was still time, and then He departed and hid Himself from them.

A sad, divine commentary is given concerning many of the people: "But though He had performed so many signs before them, yet they were not believing in Him" (v. 37). This reveals the depth of spiritual blindness that is in each person. People are not willing to reason about Jesus Christ and who He is; it takes the work of God in their hearts to cause them to realize they need Him. Apart from the convicting work of the Holy Spirit, no one sees his need of salvation. The extent of the spiritual blindness of the people is mentioned in verses 33-41.

Selfish Fear

The majority of the people refused to receive Jesus as the true Messiah. But the Bible says, "Nevertheless many even of the rulers believed in Him, but because of the Pharisees they were not confessing Him, for fear that they would be put out of the synagogue" (v. 42). Although these people feared the Pharisees and feared being excommunicated from the synagogue, notice what they really feared: "For they loved the approval of men rather than the approval of God" (v. 43). Their fear of what people would think kept them from telling others of their decision for Jesus Christ.

Pride is one of the key reasons people refuse to receive Jesus Christ as Savior. It is humiliating for a person to admit his sinful condition and his need to rely totally on someone else for salvation.

Then there is the concern about what others will think if a person makes a decision to trust Christ as Savior and to follow Him. The loss of friends is a threat to anyone.

Many who come face to face with their need of salvation refuse to trust Christ because of what they think they will have to give up. What such people fail to realize is that when they trust Jesus Christ as personal Savior, they will have new desires because they will receive a new nature. The Bible says, "Therefore if anyone is in Christ, he is a new creature; the old things passed away; behold, new things have come" (2 Cor. 5:17).

It is definitely true that after a person receives Christ as Savior some will not want to have anything to do with him. On the other hand, there will be many new friends who are also believers in Christ and have the same desire to please Christ in all they do. But in Bible times as well as today, many hold back in making decisions for Christ because they love the praise of men more than the praise of God.

Jesus and the Father

The concluding verses of John 12 reveal the relationship of Jesus with the Heavenly Father and restate the purpose Jesus had in coming to earth. Jesus said, "He who believes in Me, does not believe in Me but in Him who sent Me. He who sees Me sees the One who sent Me" (v. 44). It is not possible for a person to truly believe in the Father but not in Jesus or to truly believe in Jesus but not in the Father; the two are united.

Light for Those in Darkness

As to Jesus' purpose in coming into the world, He said, "I have come as Light into the world, so that everyone who believes in Me will not remain in darkness" (v. 46). Jesus was not referring to physical darkness but to spiritual darkness, unable to see the truth about God, himself and sin.

A time of judgment is coming for the person who rejects Jesus Christ. Jesus said, "He who rejects Me and does not receive My sayings, has one who judges him; the word I spoke is what will judge him at the last day" (v. 48).

Savior or Judge?

Jesus Christ is the standard of truth, and the Bible is His revealed Word. In order to know more about Jesus Christ, one must know more about the Bible, the written Word. But those who reject Jesus as Savior will someday be judged by the very Word they have refused to believe.

Have you trusted Jesus Christ as your personal Savior? If so, you have received forgiveness of sin and have had Christ's righteousness applied to your life. But if you have not trusted Christ as your Savior—and you pass from this life without doing so—you will be judged by Christ and by the words of truth. He has spoken. The good news, however, is that Jesus has paid the penalty for sin and that anyone who trusts Him as Savior is delivered from condemnation (John 5:24).

Study Questions

1. Why did Judas ridicule Mary's love-gift to Jesus in John 12? How do you think you would have responded if you had been there? Have you ever criticized someone for doing something "extravagant" to demonstrate their love for you of for another person? Why did it make you uncomfortable?

_____

_____

_____

_____

_____

2. Why is it so strange that the chief priests made plans to kill Lazarus? If they had succeeded in doing so, what might Jesus have done?

_____

_____

_____

_____

_____

3. What was the significance of Jesus' words "the hour has come" in John 12:23?

_____

_____

_____

_____

_____

4. Has there ever been a time when you were unwilling to yield yourself completely to God because you were afraid of what He might ask you to do? How do you feel about that situation now? How does John 12:25 relate to such a situation?

_____

_____

_____

_____

_____

5. Why did Jesus' discussion about His approaching death disturb His hearers? What had they been hoping?

_____

_____

_____

_____

_____

6. What did pride do to the Jewish leaders mentioned in John 12:43? Think of a time in your life when you struggled with pride. What conflicts did it cause for you? How did you resolve them?

_____

_____

Chapter 9 – In the Upper Room

ALTHOUGH THE FIRST 12 chapters of the Gospel of John cover the entire public ministry of the Lord Jesus—approximately three years—chapters 13-17 cover only one evening in His life. This portion has been commonly referred to as the "Upper Room Discourse."

It was time for the Feast of the Passover. This feast commemorated the time when God went throughout Egypt, passing over, or sparing, the life of the firstborn of the Israelites who had applied the blood of a lamb to their doorposts but killing the firstborn of the Egyptians, who had not applied the blood (see Ex. 12).

Jews from every locality were gathering in Jerusalem to celebrate the Feast of the Passover. "Jesus knowing that His hour had come that He would depart out of this world to the Father, having loved His own who were in the world, He loved them to the end" (John 13:1). Jesus loved His own "to the end," or literally, "to the uttermost." The love that Jesus had for his followers provides the background for all that took place at this time.

Jesus gathered with His 12 disciples in the upper room. Among them was Judas, who later betrayed Him. The events of the Last Supper reveal Jesus' love for Judas right up to the end, as well as His love for the others.

A Valuable Lesson
Even though Judas, the betrayer, was among those in the

upper room, this did not prevent Jesus from teaching His true disciples a valuable lesson. While supper was going on, He rose from His place, got a basin and towel, and began washing the disciples' feet (vv. 4-5).

At that time, it was a custom to provide water for guests to rinse their feet or to designate a servant to do this for them. Even though they may have bathed before they left home, the roads were dusty, and their feet would be dirty by the time they arrived at their destination. It was simply a courtesy on the part of a host to provide water for the guests to rinse their feet.

Although this rinsing of the feet was normally done when the guests first arrived, Jesus and His disciples were in the process of the meal when He arose and began washing their feet.

Surprised Disciples

The disciples were probably shocked at this action for two reasons—that it was being done during the meal instead of earlier and that Jesus Himself was doing it rather than designating someone else. But the fact that He Himself was washing their feet provided the lesson He wanted to teach them.

Peter refused to let Jesus wash his feet (v. 6). One can imagine Peter drawing his feet back as he resisted what the Lord was about to do. Peter said, "Never shall You wash my feet!" (v. 8). But Jesus told him, "If I do not wash you, you have no part with Me" (v. 8).

Peter's answer was a typical expression of his personality. He was impetuous and often went from one extreme to the other. He said, "Lord, then wash not only my feet, but also my hands and my head" (v. 9).

Although Peter did not want Jesus washing his feet, he was horrified at the thought of having no part with Him, so he wanted his whole body to be washed. Jesus made a distinction between words used for washing when He said, "He who has bathed needs only to wash his feet, but is completely clean;

and you are clean, but not all of you" (v. 10). The first word translated "washed" was used to refer to a complete body bath, but the second word translated "wash" referred to washing individual parts of the body.

Our Need for Cleansing

That Jesus' action and words had more significance than is seen on the surface is indicated by verse 11: "For He knew the one who was betraying Him; for this reason He said, "Not all of you are clean" Eleven of the disciples had trusted Jesus Christ as their personal Savior, so they could be referred to as being bathed and having no need for that to take place again. However, believers experience daily defilement from sin, and it is necessary for them to experience cleansing.

The Apostle John later wrote of this cleansing in his first epistle: "If we walk in the Light as He Himself is in the Light, we have fellowship with one another, and the blood of Jesus His Son cleanses us from all sin.... If we confess our sins, He is faithful and righteous to forgive us our sins and to cleanse us from all unrighteousness" (1 John 1:7, 9).

Jesus' statement that not all the disciples were clean (John 13:11) was a reference to Judas. He had not trusted Jesus as Savior; therefore, he had not been spiritually washed.

An Example for Us

Having shown the disciples the importance of humility, Jesus told them: "I gave you an example that you also should do as I did to you" (v. 15). There is divided opinion among Christians as to whether Jesus intended foot-washing to be a ceremony performed from that time forward. It seems that throughout the passage Jesus is pointing the attention of the disciples to a spiritual truth that far transcends the specific action He was performing. The specific action was related to the custom of the day, but the spiritual lesson of the need to be humble and to be a servant of others is true in any age.

As one commentator has said, "What is in view ultimately is not a ceremony of foot-washing which loses its reality where people wear shoes and walk on pavement, but a voluntary outpouring of dedicated ministry to the saints, taking whatever form is needed" (*John, A Brief Commentary,* p. 82).

Jesus Aware of Judas

Jesus told His disciples: "A slave is not greater than his master, nor is one who is sent greater than the one who sent him. If you know these things, you are blessed if you do them" (vv. 16-17). But Jesus made it known that His statement did not apply to everyone present: "I do not speak of all of you. I know the ones I have chosen; but it is that the Scripture may be fulfilled, 'HE WHO EATS MY BREAD HAS LIFTED UP HIS HEEL AGAINST ME'" (v. 18). Jesus knew what was in the heart of Judas even though none of the other disciples had an inkling of it at this time.

When Jesus said, "One of you will betray me" (v. 21), the disciples looked at each other and wondered to whom He referred. Matthew records that all of them present asked, "Surely not I, Lord?" (Matt. 26:22). Even Judas, who knew what was in his heart, asked this question (v. 25). (Of course, it would have been incriminating had Judas remained silent while everyone else was asking, "Surely not I, Lord?")

One Whom Jesus Loved

The Apostle John likely referred to himself when he said, "There was reclining on Jesus' bosom one of His disciples, whom Jesus loved" (John 13:23). The customary position at such a meal was for an individual to recline, resting on his left elbow so he could eat with his right hand. In this position, it would be possible for a person to speak to the one immediately behind him without being overheard by the others. It was in this sense that John was "reclining on Jesus' bosom."

That John was the one referred to by the words, "whom Jesus loved" is indicated by the fact that the same expression is used at other times to refer to him. John 21:20 tells that

Peter saw the "disciple whom Jesus loved," and verse 24 says, "This is the disciple who is testifying to these things and wrote these things." This indicates that mention of the disciple "whom Jesus loved" referred specifically to the Apostle John.

The Gracious Savior

At the supper, Peter caught John's attention and indicated that he should ask Jesus who was going to betray him (13:24). When John asked, Jesus said, "That is the one for whom I shall dip the morsel and give it to him" (v. 26).

This choice morsel from the meal was extended to one as a gesture of kindness. What a paradox! Judas had already determined to betray Jesus, and yet Jesus continued to treat him as a special friend. What a tremendous manifestation of the grace of God!

After Judas received the morsel he "went out immediately" (v. 30). The last words of this verse pinpoint the time as night.

A New Standard

After Jesus had left their midst, He focused His attention on the remaining 11 disciples. He told them: "A new commandment I give to you, that you love one another, even as I have loved you, that you also love one another. By this all men will know that you are My disciples, if you have love for one another" (John 13:34-35). They had been previously commanded to love (see Lev. 19:18), but they had not been specifically commanded to love "as I have loved you." This kind of love was to characterize believers from that time forward.

Paul told husbands to "love your wives, just as Christ also loved the church and gave Himself up for her" (Eph. 5:25). John 13:35 indicates that when believers love each other they display to the world that they are truly the followers of Christ.

Peter's Bold Assertion

Jesus had mentioned that He would be going away but the disciples would not be able to come after Him (v. 33). This caused Peter to ask the Lord where He was going. Jesus responded by again stating that where He was going Peter would not be able to follow now but would be able to do so later (v. 36).

Peter could not imagine why he could not follow Jesus and exclaimed, "I will lay down my life for You" (v. 37). At this time Jesus spoke those sobering words to Peter: "a rooster will not crow until you deny Me three times" (v. 38). Peter did not know his own weakness, and later during the trial of Jesus, Peter even denied that he knew Him.

Words of Assurance and Comfort

The 11 disciples were perplexed about what Jesus meant by going away. Jesus said, "Do not let your heart be troubled; believe in God, believe also in Me" (14:1). The emphasis of the original language here is: "stop letting your hearts be troubled." and notice the solution to a troubled heart: confidence in God.

Jesus explained that in His Father's house were many "dwelling places." Jesus assured them that He would come back and receive them to Himself so they would be where He is. (v. 3).

When Jesus said, "And you know the way where I am going" (v. 4), Thomas said to Him, "Lord, we do not know where You are going, how do we know the way?" (v. 5). Jesus responded by saying, "I am the way, and the truth, and the life; no one comes to the Father but through Me" (v. 6).

Jesus does not just show a person the way; He *is* the way. So also, He does not tell someone what the truth is or where to find life; He *is* the truth, and He *is* the life. No greater statements could be made that emphasize the need for a personal relationship with Jesus Christ. Because of sin, mankind needed a way back to God. Because it had believed a lie, mankind needed truth. Because it was spiritually dead, mankind needed life.

Jesus and the Father
At the mention of the Father, Philip asked Jesus to show them the Father (v. 8). Jesus explained that those who had seen Him had seen the Father (v. 9). Because Jesus was God in the flesh, He revealed the characteristics and standards of God the Father. John had recorded earlier: "No one has seen God at any time; the only begotten God who is in the bosom of the Father, He has explained Him" (1:18). Jesus was now telling Philip that because the disciples had seen Him they had seen the Father.

Jesus explained further that those who are rightly related to Him would do even greater works than He had done (14:12). In what sense could they be "greater" works? They could not be greater in extent, inasmuch as Jesus had even raised the dead (11:43-44). The works could be greater in number, however, since there would be believers all around the world who could do good works. Notice that believers' doing greater works was related to Jesus' going to His Father (14:12).

The Indwelling Comforter
Jesus said, "I will ask the Father, and He will give you another Helper, that He may be with you forever" (v. 16). Since the Holy Spirit was to come and indwell every believer, the works of believers would be greater in number than what Jesus Himself was able to do while He was one earth.

Concerning the Holy Spirit, Jesus told the disciples: "He abides with you and will be in you" (v. 17). By these words Jesus alluded to both the Old Testament and New Testament relationships of the Holy Spirit to believers.

During the Old Testament times, the Holy Spirit came upon certain believers to empower them for service. Apparently the Holy Spirit left them when the service had been performed or terminated, as indicated by David's prayer: "Do not take Your Holy Spirit from me" (Ps. 51:11). Such a prayer need not be prayed today, however, because the Scriptures reveal that the Holy Spirit comes to a person at the time of salvation and that He never leaves him (Rom. 8:9;

Eph. 1:13,14; 4:30). Although the Holy Spirit came upon many Old Testament believers to empower them for service, He did not indwell every believer until the Church Age began on the Day of Pentecost.

The Greek word translated "Helper" (John 14:16) literally means "one called alongside to help." The Holy Spirit indwells the believer and provides whatever the believer needs. At times this is encouragement; at times it is conviction of sin; at times it is special enablement for a difficult task. For whatever purpose, the Holy Spirit is the believer's divine Helper.

A New Commandment

In addition to telling his disciples about the coming of the Spirit, Jesus told them how they would know someone loves Him. "He who has My commandments and keeps them is the one who loves Me; and he who loves Me will be loved by My Father, and I will love him and will disclose Myself to him" (v. 21).

Jesus was not referring to the Old Testament Law when He mentioned "commandments" but to things He had told the disciples. In particular, in the upper room that very night He had He had told them: "A new commandment I give to you, that you love one another, even as I have loved you, that you also love one another" (13:34). Christianity is more than talk; it is right relationship with a person, Jesus Christ, and this relationship expresses itself in good works and love toward others.

The Trinity and the Believer

Although it is the special ministry of the Holy Spirit to indwell believers, Jesus made it clear that the Father and Son indwell believers as well. He said, "If anyone loves Me, he will keep My word; and My Father will love him, and We will come to him and make Our abode with him" (14:23). The Apostle Paul recognized the ministry of the indwelling Christ, for he told the Colossian believers: "Christ in you, the hope of glory" (Col. 1:27).

In the upper room Jesus mentioned again to His disciples the coming of the Holy Spirit. He told them that when the Holy Spirit comes, "He will teach you all things, and bring to your remembrance all that I said to you" (John 14:26).

There is the general principle that the Holy Spirit helps every believer to recall spiritual truths he has learned. But this verse most likely points specifically to the fact that those to whom Jesus was speaking in the upper room would be the writers of the New Testament Scriptures. As such, it would be necessary for the Holy Spirit to enable them to recall exactly the things Jesus had said so they might be accurately recorded.

Peace Amid Hostility
Even as Jesus spoke, a hostile environment surrounded His followers. The Roman government was not cordial to Christianity and later even declared it an illegal religion. In the Roman Empire Caesar was recognized as lord; therefore, Christians who recognized Jesus as Lord would not be looked upon with any favor. And in addition to this conflict, there were those at that time plotting the death of Jesus. The religious leaders had been trying to trap Him for some time, and now Judas was out somewhere furthering his plans to betray him.

Yet, in the midst of all of this, Jesus told His small band of followers: "Peace I leave with you; My peace I give to you; not as the world gives do I give to you. Do not let your heart be troubled, nor let it be fearful" (v. 27). The only peace the world knows depends on circumstances, but the peace the Christian knows depends on the confidence he has in God. The believer can have joy and peace even in the midst of adverse circumstances.

Urgency
Jesus explained that there was not much time left: "I will not speak much more with you, for the ruler of the world is

coming, and he has nothing in Me" (v. 30). "The ruler of the world" is a reference to Satan. Paul referred to him as "the god of this world" (2 Cor. 4:4), and as "the prince of the power of the air" (Eph. 2:2).

Jesus said the ruler of the world had nothing in Him. There were no means by which Satan could get a foothold in the life of Christ. This was because Jesus did not have a sin nature, so it could be said of him, "In Him there is no sin" (1 John 3:5).

Having told His disciples these things, Jesus said, "Get up, let us go from here" (John 14:31). This was the signal to leave the upper room where they had gathered for the Last Supper. The words recorded in the next chapter were spoken as the small band followed Jesus to the Garden of Gethsemane.

Study Questions

1. Some Christian fellowships today still practice literal foot-washing. If you have ever participated in a foot-washing service, how did you feel? If you have never witnessed such an event, how do you think you would feel if someone offered to wash your feet? What truth was Jesus trying to convey to His disciples through washing their feet?

_____

_____

_____

_____

_____

2. How do you respond to someone you know is seeking to discredit your life or ministry—or even seeking to harm

you physically? How did Jesus act toward Judas in comparison to how He acted toward the other disciples?

_____

_____

_____

_____

_____

3. Jesus' commandment to His disciples—and to us—is to love one another as He loved us (see John 13:34-35). In what practical ways can you demonstrate unconditional love to other believers?

_____

_____

_____

_____

_____

4. Peter made a rash promise in John 13:37. Have you ever made a promise that you failed to keep? How did you feel about your failure? How did the person to whom you had made the promise feel? How can you keep from making rash promises?

_____

_____

_____

_____

_____

5. How is it possible for Jesus' followers to do "greater works" than He Himself performed? How does the ministry of the Holy Spirit in the lives of believers today differ from His ministry in the lives of Old Testament saints?

_____

_____

_____

_____

_____

6. As you think about the physical environment at the time of Christ, what is the significance of His promise of peace? What circumstances in your life tend to threaten your peace? What steps can you take to appropriate the peace of God in your life despite your personal circumstances?

Chapter 10 – The Vine and the Branches

HAVING TOLD THE DISCIPLES, "Get up, let us go from here" (John 14:31), Jesus and the 11 left the upper room and walked to the Garden of Gethsemane. Along the way, Jesus said what is recorded in John 15.

Jesus told them, "I am the true vine, and My Father is the vinedresser. Every branch in Me that does not bear fruit, He takes away; and every branch that bears fruit, He prunes it so that it may bear more fruit" (vv. 1-2). In these statements Jesus likened his relationship with the 11 disciples to a vineyard.

Branches Dependent on the Vine
Jesus did not leave the disciples wondering about how their relationship compared to a vineyard. He identified Himself as "the true vine" (v. 1), and the Heavenly Father as "the vinedresser" (v. 1), Jesus was emphasizing fruit bearing, as indicated by the words "fruit" and "more fruit" (v. 2) and "much fruit" (v. 5). As is the case with every analogy, not every detail precisely fits the parallel that is drawn, but a main teaching can be derived from the illustration. The main teaching in this passage concerns believers and fruit bearing.

Jesus told the disciples, "You are already clean because of the word which I have spoken to you" (v. 3). Earlier in the upper room Jesus had said, "He who has bathed needs only to wash his feet, but is completely clean; and you are clean, but not all of you" (13:10). Inasmuch as Judas was not a believer,

Jesus was not able to say that all in the upper room were clean. But now, talking only to the disciples, Jesus said, "You are already clean because of the word which I have spoken to you" (15:3).

Jesus told these true believers, "Abide in Me, and I in you. As the branch cannot bear fruit of itself unless it abides in the vine, so neither can you unless you abide in Me" (v. 4). In His vineyard analogy, Jesus had identified Himself as the "vine" (v. 1), and as He talked of branches it was evident He was referring to believers. But Jesus did not leave them wondering about the identification of the branches in the analogy. He said, "I am the vine, you are the branches" (v. 5). The branches draw their life sustenance from the vine, and the fruit of the vine is produced through the branches only as they have a healthy relationship with the vine.

Fruit bearing and Salvation

In this passage, verse 2 has been the center of controversy. The statement "Every branch in Me that does not bear fruit, He takes away" has been interpreted by some to mean that the believer who does not produce fruit loses his salvation. This view is not supported by this context, however, for the subject is not salvation but fruit bearing. As indicated previously, not every detail in an analogy has to precisely fit what is illustrated.

Also, the belief that a Christian loses his salvation is not producing fruit is not supported elsewhere in the Scriptures. A believer loses rewards for lack of fruit bearing, but he does not lose his relationship with Jesus Christ. In fact, the Gospel of John earlier recorded the words of Jesus concerning the security of everyone who has trusted Him as Savior. The Lord Jesus said, "I give eternal life to them, and they will never perish; and no one will snatch them out of My hand. My Father, who has given them to Me, is greater than all; and no one is able to snatch them out of the Father's hand." (10:28-29).

The word translated "takes away" in John 15:2 can also be translated "raise" or "lift." It does not necessarily have the sense of removal but can have the meaning, especially in this context, of the care of the vinedresser as he seeks to obtain more fruit from the branches. Branches on the ground needed to be raised so they did not become covered with dirt and hinder fruit bearing.

Another possibility of interpretation of this passage is that Jesus was referring to those who had only a superficial relationship with Him but not an actual one. Judas had such a relationship. He was one of the 12 and was supposedly a true follower of Jesus, but the events of chapter 13 revealed he was not. In chapter 15 Jesus may have been referring to such people as Judas when He said, "Every branch in Me that does not bear fruit, He takes away" (v. 2). But even in this case, it was not an actual relationship that had been terminated; that is, Judas did not lose his salvation, because there never was a genuine relationship.

Making More Productive

In this passage dealing so much with fruit-bearing, Jesus stressed, "Every branch in Me that does not bear fruit, He takes away; and every branch that bears fruit, He prunes it so that it may bear more fruit" (v. 2). Notice that the Father works with the branch in such a way that it might be even more productive. This is what God desires from each person who knows Jesus Christ as personal Savior.

That the desired fruit can be produced only by one in vital relationship with Jesus Christ is seen form verse 4: "Abide in Me, and I in you. As the branch cannot bear fruit of itself unless it abides in the vine, so neither can you unless you abide in Me." The person who abides in Christ is the one who has received Him as personal Savior (1 John 4:15) and is living in fellowship with Him (3:23-24).

In this analogy of the vine and the branches, Jesus told the disciples, "He who abides in Me and I in him, he bears much fruit, for apart from Me you can do nothing" (John 15:5). It is possible to do things that the world considers significant, but nothing of eternal value can be done apart form a vital relationship with Jesus Christ. But when this relationship exists, one can say with the Apostle Paul, "I can do all things through Him who strengthens me" (Phil. 4:13).

John 15:6 has also been pointed to by some as an evidence that one can lose his salvation. Jesus said, "If anyone does not abide in Me, he is thrown away as a branch and dries up; and they gather them, and cast them into the fire and they are burned." Again, it should be stressed that every point of an analogy does not necessarily have to fit in the direct teaching being communicated. It is also possible that Jesus was here referring to people like Judas who never had a real relationship with Him. But for the believer, God's will is that he bear "much fruit" (v. 8).

Keeping His Commandments
Throughout this passage the bearing of more fruit and much fruit is the result of abiding in Jesus Christ. Jesus said, "If you keep My commandments, you will abide in My love; just as I have kept My Father's commandments and abide in His love" (v. 10). The one who knows Jesus Christ as Savior wants to do what Jesus reveals in His Word.

The "commandments" to which Jesus referred (v. 10), were not the Ten Commandments of the Mosaic Law but the things He had specifically told the disciples Himself. In particular. He said, "This is My commandment, that you love one another, just as I have loved you" (v. 12). Earlier He had told them: "By this all men will know that you are My disciples, if you have love for one another" (13:35). The word translated "love" in both of these passages refers to a love that seeks the highest good of others regardless of their response. It is not an emotional type of love but a love that results from an act of the will, whereby a person determines to do what is best for others.

Chosen to Be Fruitful

Throughout the first part of John 15 there are many references to fruit. In verse 16 Jesus said, "You did not choose Me but I chose you, and appointed you that you would go and bear fruit, and that your fruit would remain, so that whatever you ask of the Father in My name He may give to you." The question that arises from this and other references is "What is meant by 'fruit'?"

Fruit is the evidence of life that is produced when a branch is in a living relationship with the vine. What kind of evidence reveals that a person is in a living relationship with Jesus Christ? It is not necessarily the way a person dresses or even what he does; rather it is the characteristics of his life. These characteristics are referred to in Galatians 5:22-23 as "the fruit of the Spirit" which is "love, joy, peace, patience, kindness, goodness, faithfulness, gentleness, self-control." This fruit is the evidence of an individual's living relationship with Jesus Christ. When the fruit of the Spirit is produced through a person's life, there are lasting effects. Those who evidence this fruit will be used of the Lord in presenting the gospel to others and in encouraging believers in the faith.

In the World but Not of it

Having told His disciples about the importance of loving others, Jesus spoke sobering words to them about how they could expect to be treated by the world. He reminded them that if the world hated them, they should remember that it hated Him also (John 15:18). He told them why they should not be loved by the world: "If you were of the world, the world would love its own; but because you are not of the world, but I chose you out of the world, because of this the world hates you" (v. 19).

Believers are *in* the world, but they are not *of* the world; that is, the world is not the source of their origin because they have been born of God. Because Christians live with eternity's values in view, they are often misunderstood and sometimes persecuted by unbelievers. Christians are sometimes guilty of seeking to be friends with the world so they will not be disliked. However, the Bible says emphatically, "Do you not know that friendship with the world is hostility toward God? Therefore whoever wishes to be a friend of the world makes himself an enemy of God" (James 4:4).

Opposition Likely

Although the 11 disciples might have thought it was unfair for the world to treat them unkindly, the Lord Jesus said, "Remember the word that I said to you, 'A slave is not greater than his master.' If they persecuted Me, they will also persecute you; if they kept My word, they will keep yours also" (John 15:20). Those who know Jesus Christ as Savior should not be surprised when the world strongly opposes what they believe. If Jesus Christ were living on earth today, the world would mistreat Him just as it did before, and his servants should not expect to be treated better than He was.

For those who wonder why the world has such animosity toward Christians, Jesus answered the question when He said, "All these things they will do to you for My name's sake, because they do not know the One who sent Me" (v. 21). Jesus was mistreated because people did not know God and were not in right relationship to the Heavenly Father. This is the same reason believers are mistreated and misunderstood today.

Notice that Jesus said, "All these things they will do to you for My name's sake" (v. 21). Sometimes Christians are criticized and persecuted because of their inconsistent behavior or because of not really caring about others. Such believers are not being persecuted for the sake of Christ. The Bible says, "For what credit is there if, when you sin and are harshly treated, you endure it with patience? But if when you do what is right and suffer for it you patiently endure it, this finds favor with God" (1 Peter 2:20).

Hatred of Christ

The rulers of the Jews claimed to love God, yet they hated Jesus Christ. But the Lord Jesus said, "He who hates Me hates My Father also" (John 15:23). Many people today do not give the Lord Jesus Christ proper honor. Some do not believe that Jesus Christ is God; thus, they make Him less that God. However, the Jews of New Testament times clearly understood that Jesus was claiming to be equal with god (5:18). Those who dishonor Christ by making Him anything less than what the Bible teaches also dishonor the Father.

Jesus recognized that His rejection by mankind was the fulfillment of prophecy. He said, "They have done this to fulfill the word that is written in their Law, 'They hated Me without a cause'" (15:25). The term "law" was a common way of referring to the Old Testament Scriptures. Here, the specific reference was the psalms (see Ps, 35:19; 69:4). There was no reason for the Jews to hate Jesus Christ. If they were truly concerned about the Law they would have recognized that He was the fulfillment of it.

The Spirit of Truth

The Holy Spirit does not attract attention to Himself; rather, He focuses attention on the Lord Jesus Christ. Jesus made this clear when He said, "He will testify about Me" (v. 26). The greatest evidence that the Holy Spirit has done His work in a believer's life is that the believer has Jesus Christ as the focal point of his life. Although it is important to know about the Person and work of the Holy Spirit, Christians are not to focus their attention on the Spirit but on Christ.

Not only would the Holy Spirit witness concerning Christ, but the disciples would do this also. Jesus said, "You will testify also, because you have been with Me from the beginning" (v. 27). These 11 men were highly qualified witnesses because they had been with Jesus from the beginning of His public ministry. They would be able to relate both orally and in writing what Jesus Christ said and did. Their testimony concerning the Person and work of Jesus

Christ formed what was known as "the apostles' teaching" (Acts 2:42).

Before God's written revelation was completed, the word of the apostles was binding on believers because they spoke as authoritative representatives of the Lord Jesus Christ. Although the apostles have passed off the scene, God's Word in written form is still with us. We are no longer to look to men but to the written Word of God as the final source of authority. Anyone can safely trust himself to the authority of the Scriptures because "All Scripture is inspired by God and profitable for teaching, for reproof, for correction, for training in righteousness" (2 Tim. 3:16).

Study Questions
1. Some people claim that John 15:2 teaches that a believer can lose his salvation. Based on this lesson, what two possible interpretations of this verse would refute such a claim? Please explain.

_____

_____

_____

_____

_____

2. In John 15, Jesus explained that God desires believers to be fruitful. Read Galatians 5:22-23 for a list of "spiritual fruit." Is this fruit of the Spirit evident in your life? Which areas need more work? What can you do to further develop these areas of your life?

_____

_____

_____

_____

_____

3. Many times today we hear about Christians whose
    "rights" have been "violated" in schools, in the
    workplace, in the political arena. How should we expect
    to be treated by the unbelieving world? Why?

_____

_____

_____

_____

_____

4. A number of religious groups claim to love God while
    they deny the person and work of Jesus Christ. Why are
    such views inconsistent? What did Jesus say about such
    people?

_____

_____

_____

_____

_____

5. Of whom did Jesus say the Holy Spirit would testify? What does this suggest to you about groups today who call a great deal of attention to the activity of the Holy Spirit? Whose work should they be emphasizing?

_____

_____

_____

_____

_____

_____

_____

_____

_____

Chapter 11 – Jesus Prepares His Disciples and Prays

HAVING TOLD THE DISCIPLES that they would be persecuted by the world, Jesus said, "These things I have spoken to you so that you may be kept from stumbling. They will make you outcasts from the synagogue, but an hour is coming for everyone who kills you to think that he is offering service to God" (John 16:1-2). The Lord did not leave the impression that the disciples would have no problems now that they were in right relationship to Him. He warned them of extremely difficult times ahead. He had assured them earlier, however, that He would send the Holy Spirit to be their divine helper in every situation.

Warning Disciples
The disciples had been part of the Jewish worship of their day, but Christ warned that they would be driven form the Jewish synagogues and that those who killed them would actually think they were serving God.

Before his conversion the Apostle Paul thought he served God by persecuting Christians and even by having them put to death. Commonly known as "Saul" before his conversion, he was "ravaging the church, entering house after house; and dragging off men and women, he would put them in prison" (Acts 8:3). Paul was converted on the road to Damascus, but even his purpose for going there was to search for Christians and to bring them captive to Jerusalem (9:1-2). After his conversion Paul said, "I am a Jew, born in Tarsus of Cilicia, but brought up in this city, educated under Gamaliel, strictly according to the law of our fathers, being zealous for God just as you all are today. I persecuted this Way to the death, binding and putting both men and women into prisons" (22:3-4).

So Christ's predictions came true concerning those who would seek to kill the disciples and would even think they were serving God by doing so. Jesus told the disciples that He had not mentioned these things earlier because He was with them (John 16:4), but now that He was going away, He wanted to warn them about these matters.

The Holy Spirit's Convincing
Because the disciples were troubled, Jesus again told them that after He left them, He would send the Holy Spirit. He then told them what the Holy Spirit's ministry would be; "And He, when He comes, will convict the world concerning sin and righteousness and judgment" (v. 8).

Even though unbelievers might say they are not concerned about spiritual matters, verse 8 indicates that they are actually convinced by the Holy Spirit of sin, righteousness and judgment, The following verses specify what is involved in the Spirit's convincing in these areas. Jesus said that unbelievers, or the world, are convinced by the Holy Spirit of their sin "because they do not believe in Me" (v. 9). The Spirit's ministry is not primarily to convince an unbeliever that specific acts he does are sin but to convince him that he has rejected Jesus Christ. Jesus said the Holy Spirit would convince the world of righteousness "because I go to the Father and you no longer see Me."

Jesus said the Holy Spirit convinces the world concerning judgment "because the ruler of this world has been judged" (v. 11). Jesus was speaking these words before going to the cross, but the judgment of Satan by Christ's death on the cross was so certain that He spoke of it as an accomplished fact.

Hebrews 2:14 tells of the judgment that Christ brought on Satan at the cross: "Since the children share in flesh and blood, He Himself likewise also partook of the same, that through death He might render powerless him who had the power of death, that is, the devil." Although unbelievers may give the impression that they do not think there is anything to fear in the future, John 16:11 reveals that the Holy Spirit convinces them of coming judgment.

Guided by the Spirit

Jesus further explained to the disciples what the ministry of the Holy Spirit would be when He came. Jesus told them, "He will guide you into all the truth; for He will not speak on His own initiative, but whatever He hears, He will speak; and He will disclose to you what is to come" (John 16:13).

Earlier, Jesus had told the disciples that everything He had said to them would be recalled to their memories by the Holy Spirit (14:26). Now Jesus told them that the Holy Spirit would guide them "into all the truth" (16:13). Inasmuch as the 11 disciples were the official representatives of Jesus Christ, it was necessary for this ministry of the Spirit to be realized so they could accurately communicate Jesus' teaching to the world.

Although many believers focus attention on the Holy Spirit, Jesus made it clear that the Holy Spirit does not want this kind of attention. Jesus said, "He will glorify Me, for He will take of Mine and will disclose it to you" (v. 14). The ministry of the Holy Spirit is to cause the believer to turn his eyes on Jesus. The greatest evidence that the Holy Spirit has done His work in the believer's life is that the individual has a hunger to know more about Jesus Christ and a desire to please Him in everything he does.

As Christians study the Scriptures, God's written Word, the Holy Spirit illuminates the Scriptures and helps believers understand, the spiritual truths. This is a fulfillment of what Christ promised the disciples (v. 14).

Sorrow to Turn to Joy

As Jesus talked to the disciples about His going away, they were extremely perplexed and did not understand what He was saying (vv. 16-18). Again, Jesus reminded them of sorrow ahead when He said, "You will weep and lament, but the world will rejoice; you will grieve, but your grief will be turned into joy" (v. 20).

The disciples had followed Jesus because they were convinced He was Israel's Messiah, but now He was going away, and they would go through a time of tremendous sorrow. Jesus reminded them, however, that their sorrow would not be lasting because they would see Him again and their sorrow would turn to joy (v. 20). After Jesus' death on the cross, the disciples went through a time of terrible sorrow, but when He appeared to them after His resurrection, they had unrestrained joy.

Jesus indicated that the joy the disciples would have later would be so great it would cause them to forget their sorrow, even as a mother's joy over a newborn child causes her to forget the sorrow of childbirth (v. 21).

Direct Access to the Father

Jesus then told the disciples about the way their needs would be met after He was gone. They would go through sorrow and then experience joy when they saw Him again. Jesus told them, "In that day you will not question Me about anything. Truly, truly, I say to you, if you ask the Father for anything in My name, He will give it to you. Until now you have asked for nothing in My name; ask and you will receive, so that your joy may be made full" (vv. 23-24).

Through what Jesus was about to accomplish on the cross, He would enable every believer to have direct access to the Father. However, that access would be "in [His] name" (v. 24); that is, on the basis of what he had accomplished on the cross. Matthew 27:51 indicates that direct access to the Father was possible after Christ's death on the cross. After Jesus finished the work of redemption on the cross, "the veil of the temple was torn in two from top to bottom."

Since believers now have direct access to the Father because of what Christ accomplished on the cross, the Bible says, "Let us draw near with confidence to the throne of grace, so that we may receive mercy and find grace to help in time of need" (Heb. 4:16).

Disciples Who Understood

Jesus explained to the disciples that He had been speaking to them "in figurative language" (John 16:25), but the time would come when He would speak plainly to them concerning these matters. He again assured them that He had come from the Father into the world and that He was leaving the world to return to the Father (v. 28). His disciples clearly understood His words now, and they said, "Now we know that You know all things, and have no need for anyone to question You; by this we believe that You came from God (v. 30).

Jesus responded, "Do you now believe? Behold, an hour is coming, and has already come, for you to be scattered, each to his own home, and to leave Me alone; and yet I am not alone, because the Father is with Me" (vv. 31-32). Jesus was referring to what would happen after He would be betrayed by Judas and arrested. Both Matthew and Mark record that all of the disciples forsook Him and fled (Matt. 26:56; Mark 14:50). But even though He predicted this would happen, Jesus assured the disciples He would not be alone because the Heavenly Father was with Him (John 16:32).

Jesus then again stated to the disciples what they could expect from an unbelieving world: "These things I have spoken to you, so that in Me you may have peace. In the world you have tribulation, but take courage; I have overcome the world" (v. 33).

Although the disciples would find extreme difficulty as long as they lived in the world and took a stand for Christ, they could have a peace that passes understanding because they were in right relationship to Him. This reveals that a believer's peace does not depend on external circumstances but on his relationship with Jesus Christ.

Our Lord's Prayer

The Apostle John recorded: "Jesus spoke these things; and lifting up His eyes to heaven, He said, "Father, the hour has come; glorify Your Son, that the Son may glorify You" (17:1). The prayer recorded in John 17 was truly the Lord's prayer. The prayer so commonly referred to as the Lord's prayer (Matt. 6:9-13) was actually only a model prayer for the disciples and was not one that the Lord Jesus Himself prayed.

As Jesus and His disciples were on the way to the Garden of Gethsemane, He prayed for Himself (John 17:1-5), for his disciples (vv. 6-19), and for all believers (vv. 20-26). Jesus prayed that the Father would glorify Him so that in turn He might glorify the Father (v. 1). Just as the Holy Spirit desires to focus attention on Christ (16:14), the Lord Jesus Christ, while He was on earth, constantly focused attention on the Heavenly Father.

How one comes into right relationship with God is seen from the words Jesus spoke to the Father: "This is eternal life, that they may know You, the only true God, and Jesus Christ whom You have sent" (17:3). A person does not receive eternal life by doing certain works but by knowing and believing in the Father and the Son. This implies, of course, that one believes what the Scriptures say about these Persons. To believe what the Scriptures say means a person realizes he is a sinner and has come short of God's glory (Rom. 3:23), that he is unable to be saved by works (Eph. 2:8-9), that only Christ has paid the penalty for sin (Rom. 3:25; I Cor. 15:3), and that he must personally receive Christ as his Savior (John 1:12).

Christ's Glory

In His prayer to the Father, Jesus said, "I glorified You on the earth, having accomplished the work which You have given Me to do. Now, Father, glorify Me together with Yourself, with the glory which I had with You before the world was"

(17:4-5). Jesus here referred to His relationship with the Father before creation and before He took upon Himself a human body.

Philippians 2:5-8 tells of Christ's willingness to give up the glory He had with the Father to come to earth and die on the cross for the sins of the world. "Although He existed in the form of God, did not regard equality with God a thing to be grasped, but emptied Himself, taking the form of a bond-servant, and being made in the likeness of men" (vv. 6-7).

Jesus did not give up being God by coming to earth, but He willingly gave up the right to independently express His divine attributes. Although there were occasional times when, under the direction of the Father, Jesus manifested His divine attributes while on earth (see John 1:50; 2:24), He also experienced the limitations of a human body (4:6-7). As Jesus talked to the Heavenly Father in prayer, He asked for His original glory to be restored.

Prayer for His Disciples
Having prayed concerning Himself, Jesus then prayed for the disciples. He told the Father, "The words which You gave Me I have given to them; and they received them and truly understood that I came forth from You, and they believed that You sent Me" (17:8). Jesus distinctly stated that He was praying for the disciples, not for unbelievers: "I ask on their behalf; I do not ask on behalf of the world, but of those whom You have given Me; for they are Yours" (v. 9).

At the time, Jesus was concerned about His disciples; thus, He was praying for them and not for the world. Some have taken this to mean that believers are never to pray for the world, but the Scriptures clearly state elsewhere that believers are to pray for "all men" (I Tim. 2:1), which definitely includes unbelievers.

As Jesus prayed, He was concerned that the Father keep the disciples that had been given to Him. Jesus knew that the Father could do this, because earlier He had said that no one was able to snatch believers out of the Father's hand (John

10:28-29).

In telling the Father that He had kept the disciples while He was in the world, Jesus said, "Not one of them perished but the son of perdition, so that the Scripture would be fulfilled" (17:12). Judas had never come into a right relationship with Jesus Christ but had continually opposed Him. This was in fulfillment of Psalm 41:9: "Even my close friend in whom I trusted, who ate my bread, has lifted up his heel against me."

Jesus said He had given God's Word to the disciples, and this was why the world had hated them (John 17:14). They had believed the message of God, so they were despised by an unbelieving world. Jesus did not pray that the disciples would be removed from the world and thereby escape all persecutions. He said, "I do not ask You to take them out of the world, but to keep them from the evil one" (v. 15).

In the original language, the world "evil" is in the masculine gender; thus, the word "person" or "one" should be supplied. The evil one to whom Christ referred was the Devil, earlier described as "the ruler of this world" (16:11). Although the disciples were in the world they were not of the world; that is, their origin was not of the world system but of God, because they had trusted Christ as Savior.

Set Apart to God
In this day of concern as to how believers can be more separated to God, Jesus' words to the father are highly significant: "Sanctify them in the truth; Your word is truth" (v. 17). The word "sanctify" refers to that which is "set apart." Just as in the pagan religions of the time, certain things were set apart to the worship of the false gods, so believers in Jesus Christ are to be set apart to the true God. This is embodied in His Word, now available in written form.

Believers are to study the Word of God to learn more about Jesus Christ and then to put into practice what the Word reveals.

As He prayed, Jesus told the Father that he was sending

the disciples into the world just as He had been sent by the Father into the world (John 17:18). Then Jesus reiterated His concern that the disciples "may be sanctified in truth" (v. 19).

Prayer for All Believers
After praying for Himself and for the disciples, Jesus then prayed for all believers. He said, "I do not ask on behalf of these alone, but for those also who believe in Me through their word" (v. 20). Having believed in Him, the disciples were responsible to declare the message so others would believe on Jesus Christ.

Jesus' concern for those who believed in Him as Savior was "that they may all be one; even as You, Father, are in Me and I in You, that they also may be in Us, so that the world may believe that You sent Me" (v. 21). The oneness to which Jesus referred does not require organizational unity. There is no indication in the Scriptures that all believers are to be united in a single organization.

Jesus was concerned about spiritual unity and that believers display this unity to an unbelieving world. He indicated that unity of believers has an evangelizing effect on the world: "that the world may believe that You sent Me" (v. 21). Believers who are unable to get along with each other do not present a convincing message about Jesus Christ to an unbelieving world.

The Indwelling Savior
Although it is common to refer to the fact that the Holy Spirit indwells believers (I Cor. 6:19-20), it is evident from Christ's words that the Father and the Son also indwell every believer. Jesus said, "I in them and You in Me, that they may be perfected in unity, so that the world may know that You sent Me, and loved them, even as You have loved Me" (John 17:23). Colossians 1:27 also reveals that Christ indwells every believer: "Christ in you, the hope of glory."

Earlier Jesus had told the disciples that He was going away but that He would come back again and take them to be with

Him (John 14:3). In His prayer to the Father, Jesus said, "Father, I desire that they also, whom You have given Me, be with Me where I am, so that they may see My glory which You have given Me, for You loved Me before the foundation of the world" (17:24).

Jesus concluded His prayer to the Father by saying, "I have made Your name known to them, and will make it known, so that the love with which You loved Me may be in them, and I in them" (v. 26).

John 17 is commonly referred to as Jesus' high-priestly prayer. He was interceding not only for Himself but also for the disciples and for all who would later believe on Him as Savior.

Study Questions

1. In John 16:8-11 Jesus explained how the Holy Spirit would minister to unbelievers. What do these verses tell you about those who say they don't believe there is anything wrong with their lives and that they have no concern about spiritual matters?

_____

_____

_____

_____

_____

2. According to this lesson, what is the greatest evidence that the Holy Spirit has done His work in the believer's life? Does your life show that the Holy Spirit has been at work in you? If not, why?

_____

_____

_____

_____

_____

3. What does it mean to you to have direct access to the Father? If you have not recently thanked the Lord Jesus for making that possible, why not do so now?

_____

_____

_____

_____

_____

4. Read carefully Jesus' prayer recorded in John 17. Make a chart, listing the different individuals and groups for whom He prayed and the specific requests He made for them. During your devotional time this week, meditate on these requests. How can you incorporate some of these into your prayer life?

_____

_____

_____

_____

_____

5. Explain what it means to you personally that Jesus prayed for *you* before He went to the cross and that He intercedes today on *your* behalf.

_____

_____

_____

_____

_____

_____

_____

_____

_____

_____

Chapter 12 - Jesus Arrested and Tried

THE EVENTS RECORDED IN John 13-17 took place during the evening and nighttime. John specified that when Judas left the group "it was night" (13:30).

Jesus and the 11 disciples stayed in the upper room for a time and then made their way toward the Garden of Gethsemane. That which is recorded in John 15-17 took place the same night, while Jesus and the 11 were on their way to the garden.

In the Garden of Gethsemane

John 18:1 says, "When Jesus had spoken these words, He went forth with His disciples." The expression "these words" refers to Jesus' high-priestly prayer, recorded in chapter 17.

The garden is not specifically named in the Gospel of John, but it is identified as the Garden of Gethsemane in Matthew 26:36 and Mark 14:32. As John indicates, it was place where Jesus and His disciples had frequently met, so Judas knew where to look for them (John 18:2).

In the darkness of the night, Judas came to the garden "having received the Roman cohort and officers from the chief priests and the Pharisees, came there with lanterns and torches and weapons" (v. 3). The specific number of those who came with Judas is not mentioned, but it is evident that there were enough to take Jesus captive regardless of the opposition He and the disciples might have given.

Surprised Men

Because it was night and the men with Judas might have to search for Jesus before they could overpower Him by force, they came "with lanterns and torches and weapons" (v. 3). If they were expecting a long search for Jesus, they were surprised because "Jesus, knowing all the things that were coming upon Him, went forth and said to them, 'Whom do you seek?'" (v. 4). When they answered, "Jesus the Nazarene" (v. 5), Jesus told them, "I am He" (v. 5). As soon as He said, "I am He," the group of men drew back and fell to the ground (v. 6).

How strange! Those who came prepared to take Jesus captive by force actually gave Him opportunity to escape by drawing back and falling to the ground. Although the Scriptures do not say why they reacted in this way, it is possible that they responded like this because of His statement "I am He." In the original language, there is no word here for "He"; rather, there is only the statement, "I am." This expression is related to the way God revealed Himself to Moses (see Ex. 3:14), so it is possible that the would-be captors responded in this way because they were conditioned to reverence the name of God.

Instead of making any attempt to excuse, Jesus asked them again, "Whom do you seek?" (v. 7). Before this armed group, Jesus again identified Himself and then spoke in behalf of the disciples. He said, "I told you that I am He; so if you seek Me, let these go their way" (v. 8). Again, the "He" is not in the original.

Hasty, Bold Peter

Peter, typical of his impetuous nature, "having a sword, drew it and struck the high priest's slave, and cut off his right ear; and the slave's name was Malchus" (v. 10). The Scriptures do not explain why Peter happened to have a sword. The other Gospel writers do not mention Peter by name, perhaps because they wrote while he was still alive and naming him could have brought reprisals on him. However, John—who wrote at the end of the first century, after Peter's death, singled him out as the one who cut off the ear of the high priest's servant.

Whatever was lacking in Peter's character, he certainly was not lacking in courage at this time. Surely he realized the great odds the disciples and Jesus faced against this band of armed men, but he did not cower in their presence.

Jesus told Peter, "Put the sword into the sheath" (v. 11). Luke, the physician, mentioned in his Gospel that Jesus healed the servant's ear (Luke 22:51), but John hastened on in his account to explain what followed this incident.

Jesus asked, "The cup which the Father has given Me, shall I not drink it?" (v. 11). His question to Peter indicated that His hour had come to allow Himself to be captured and crucified for the sin of the world.

Jesus Bound and Taken

Jesus had frequently escaped those who had attempted to seize Him before this, for His hour had not come. Not wanting to take any chances of His escaping, the band of armed men bound Him before leading Him off (John 18:12). Then they "led Him to Annas first; for he was father-in-law of Caiaphas, who was high priest that year" (v. 13). Jesus was probably taken to Annas first because, even though Annas was no longer high priest, he was highly respected because of his previous position in this office. Also, he still had influence as the father-in-law of the present high priest. It is also possible that Annas was even at this time presiding over the Sanhedrin, the Jewish supreme court.

John went on to explain, "Now Caiaphas was the one who had advised the Jews that it was expedient for one man to die on behalf of the people" (v. 14). John was referring to an incident he had recorded earlier concerning complaints against Christ (11:47-53). Caiaphas was high priest during Jesus' entire public ministry. The Jews who took Jesus captive wanted to have a speedy trial even though it was in the middle of the night, so He was taken first to Annas and then to Caiaphas.

At the High Priest's Palace

At this point in his account, John told of Peter and another disciple who went with Jesus when He was taken to the high priest. "Simon Peter was following Jesus, and so was another disciple. Now that disciple was known to the high priest, and entered with Jesus into the court of the high priest" (v. 15). The words "another disciple" are probably a reference to the Apostle John himself, as it was not his custom to refer to himself by name.

John wrote that the group went into the palace, probably meaning the palace courtyard. While Peter was in the courtyard, a girl who was on duty at the door asked him, "You are not also one of this man's disciples, are you?" (v. 17). Peter gave a short, clear answer: "I am not" (v. 17).

Patient Under Questioning

Meanwhile, inside the palace the high priest was questioning Jesus about His teaching. Jesus explained that He had taught publicly, particularly in the synagogue, so there was no secret about what He taught. Jesus told the high priest: "Why do you question Me? Question those who have heard what I spoke to them; they know what I said" (v. 21). Although the Jews were trying to hastily condemn Jesus on false charges, this answer made it clear there were many people who knew what His true teaching was.

Jesus' answer made one of the officers angry. And he struck Jesus with the palm of his hand, saying, "Is that the way You answer the high priest?" (v. 22). But then Jesus put the burden of proof on the officer by saying, "If I have spoken wrongly, testify of the wrong; but if rightly, why do you strike Me?" (v. 23).

No evidence could be brought forth to show that Jesus spoke anything other than the truth. Since nothing significant was being accomplished at this trial, "Annas sent Him bound to Caiaphas the high priest" (v. 24). Annas and Caiaphas probably lived in different quarters in the same house.

Peter's Denial
Peter was still outside in the courtyard trying to keep warm in the early morning hours. Those with him said, "You are not also one of His disciples, are you?" (v. 25). A second time Peter responded with a short clear answer: "I am not" (v. 25).

At this time a servant, a relative of the servant whose ear Peter had cut off, asked, "Did I not see you in the garden with Him?" (v. 26). For the third time Peter denied any association with the Lord, "and immediately a rooster crowed" (v. 27).

Earlier, when Peter had assured Jesus: "I will lay down my life for You" (13:37), Jesus had told him: "Will you lay down your life for Me? Truly, truly, I say to you, a rooster will not crow until you deny Me three times" (v. 38). So Peter's third denial and the crowing of the rooster fulfilled precisely what Jesus had said would happen.

In Pilate's Judgment Hall
In his account John quickly moved on to the next event: "Then they led Jesus from Caiaphas into the Praetorium, and it was early; and they themselves did not enter into the Praetorium so that they would not be defiled, but might eat the Passover" (18:28). For a full account of all that took place during the betrayal, arrest, trial, and crucifixion of Jesus, one needs to consult all four of the Gospel accounts.

John quickly proceeded to tell what happened as Jesus was brought before the representatives of the Roman government in the early morning hours, probably between 3:00 and 6:00 a.m. Since a Gentile, Pilate, was involved, the Jews did not go into the judgment hall, because they did not want to defile themselves. The following account reveals Pilate going back and forth between Jesus in the judgment hall and the Jews on the outside.

Since Pilate had been appointed by the Roman Emperor as the Governor of Judea, there had been much animosity between him and the Jews. At various times, Pilate had offended the Jews to the extent that he nearly drove them to insurrection. On one occasion, he even appropriated revenue from the temple to build an aqueduct. Luke 13:1 indicates that he was also responsible for the death of some Galileans while they were offering sacrifices.

Determined Pilate

Although the Jews strongly disliked Pilate, they despised Jesus so bitterly that they came to Pilate for help in getting Him condemned. Pilate asked the Jews, "What accusation do you bring against this Man?" (18:29).

The Jews avoided giving a direct answer by saying, "If this Man were not an evildoer, we would not have delivered Him to you" (v. 30). They had hoped Pilate would condemn Jesus quickly, without even seeking evidence to support any guilt.

Pilate refused to have anything to do with that kind of action, so he told the Jews, "Take Him yourselves, and judge Him according to your law" (v. 31). Pilate probably did not want to be bothered by these Jews whom he had such little concern for. He likely thought this was some religious squabble they should handle on their own without involving the Roman government.

The intent of the accusers was evident, however, when they told Pilate: "We are not permitted to put anyone to death" (v. 31). The Roman government had the full authority over capital punishment in all of the provinces under its control. The Jews were determined to put Jesus to death but were not able to do so unless the Roman government approved it.

Pilate Questioning Jesus

Pilate then turned from the Jews outside the judgment hall and went inside the hall to talk to Jesus. He asked Jesus, "Are You the King of the Jews?" (v. 33). Pilate actually put the emphasis on the word "You"; thus, it could be translated: "You are the King of the Jews?" It was as if Pilate could not imagine that the Person before him would be making any claim at all about being King of the Jews.

Instead of answering directly, Jesus asked Pilate: "Are you saying this on your own initiative, or did others tell you about Me?" (v. 34). Pilate did not specifically answer Jesus' question but said, "I am not a Jew, am I? Your own nation and the chief priests delivered You to me; what have You done?" (v. 35). The accusers should have given specific charges and provided evidence supporting their charges, but since they had not, Pilate asked Jesus Himself what He had done.

An Unworldly Kingdom

A king is one who reigns over a kingdom, and Jesus explained to Pilate that His kingdom was not of this world (v. 36). Jesus supported this claim by saying, "If My kingdom were of this world, then My servants would be fighting so that I would not be handed over to the Jews; but as it is, My kingdom is not of this realm?" (v. 36).

This was more than Pilate could understand. If a person's kingdom were not of this world, he did not understand how that person could be a king. So he asked Jesus, "So You are a king?" (v. 37). Jesus not only gave an affirmative answer to Pilate, but He also explained that this was the whole purpose of His coming to earth. Jesus said, "You say correctly that I am a king. For this I have been born, and for this I have come into the world, to testify to the truth. Everyone who is of the truth hears My voice" (v. 37).

Earlier, Jesus had said that those who were not His own would not hear His voice, although His own would. He said, "My sheep hear My voice, and I know them, and they follow Me" (10:27). In the words Jesus spoke to Pilate, it is apparent that the ones Jesus referred to as hearing His voice were those who believed in Him as Savior. Jesus emphasized that He was testifying "to the truth" (18:37) and said, "Everyone who is of the truth hears My voice" (v. 37).

Pilate was specifically trying to find out what the charges were against Jesus and whether or not He was guilty. Jesus' comments about the truth probably seemed unrelated to the subject at hand. Pilate reflected the attitude of the unbelieving world when he said, "What is truth?" (v. 38). Pilate did not realize that the One standing in front of him at the moment was the embodiment of the truth. Jesus had said earlier, "I am the way, and the truth, and the life; no one comes to the Father but through Me" (14:6).

A Choice Given

Without waiting for an answer, Pilate turned from Jesus to talk to the Jews waiting outside. He told them, "I find no guilt in Him (18:38). Although Pilate did not understand what Jesus was saying about truth, he realized there was no reason to put Him to death as the Jews were asking him to do.

Pilate then gave the Jews a choice: "But you have a custom that I release someone for you at the Passover; do you wish then that I release for you the King of the Jews? (v. 39). Pilate might have thought he could get out of his dilemma by capitalizing on the custom of releasing a prisoner each year at Passover time. Pilate probably thought the Jews would prefer Jesus to a known criminal but, if so, he misjudged the situation. Because of the Jews' hatred of Jesus, they cried out, "Not this Man, but Barabbas" (v. 40).

John added the statement: "Now Barabbas was a robber" (v. 40). Although this is all that John said of Barabbas, Mark recorded: "The man named Barabbas had been imprisoned with the insurrectionists who had committed murder in the insurrection" (Mark 15:7). Not only was Barabbas a robber, but he was also a known murderer; yet the Jews preferred that he be released and Jesus be put to death.

The Most Important Question

The Jews had decided what they wanted to do with Jesus; nothing could deter them. Every person must inwardly answer the question: "What will you do with Jesus?" Those who recognize Him as the Son of God and the Savior of the world receive forgiveness of sins and eternal life by trusting in Him for salvation (John 3:16; 5:24). Those who refuse Him as Savior remain in their state of condemnation (3:18). What will you do with Jesus?

Study Questions

1. What is the literal meaning of the phrase "I am He" in John 18:5, 8? Why did this response from Jesus startle His would be captors?

---

2. It is easy for us, many years removed from the situation, to condemn Peter for his cowardly denial of Jesus. But as you reflect on your Christian life, can you think of a time when you denied the Lord either verbally or through silence? How did you feel about it later? What could you have said or done instead to be a better witness?

---

3. Notice the inconsistency on the part of the Jewish leaders who were pressing for a hasty and false judgment against Jesus but who wouldn't enter the judgment hall because they didn't want to be defiled. What inconsistencies do you find in your life? How do you intend to remedy them?

_____

_____

_____

_____

_____

4. Why did Pilate not understand Jesus' comments about His kingdom? How can you explain to someone the kingdom of God when it is so intangible?

_____

_____

_____

_____

_____

5. Explain the continuing significance of the question, What will you do with Jesus? (see Matt. 27:22; Mark 15:12). How have you personally answered that question in your life?

_____

_____

_____

_____

_____

_____

_____

_____

_____

_____

_____

_____

_____

Chapter 13 – Jesus Condemned, Crucified, Buried

AFTER QUESTIONING JESUS, PILATE had told the Jews, "I find no guilt in Him" (John 18:38). But even so, the Jews preferred having one released to them who was guilty of robbery and murder, rather than Jesus (Mark 15:7; John 18:39-40).

The Scourging

Although he could find no evidence to support any charge the Jews had made, or might make, against Christ, "Pilate then took Jesus and scourged Him" (19:1). It is strange that Pilate had one he considered innocent scourged, but apparently it was to arouse sympathy among the Jews so they would want Jesus released. Scourging was a severe punishment that was usually inflicted by a whip with leather thongs that often had stones and pieces of metal in their tips. Some died from such severe beatings. Even the Roman Empire considered this punishment to be so severe that its citizens were protected from it.

The Roman soldiers were much more than willing to participate in abusing Jesus. There was much animosity between the Roman government and the Jews, and this provided the Romans with another opportunity to ridicule one who was a Jew, according to the flesh. "The soldiers twisted together a crown of thorns and put it on His head, and put a purple robe on Him; and they began to come up to Him and say, "Hail, King of the Jews!" and to give Him slaps in the face (vv. 2-3).

Jesus underwent this brutal punishment willingly because it was part of God's plan leading up to His redemptive work on the cross. Because He was God as well as man, Jesus could have brought judgment on those Roman soldiers at any moment had He chosen to do so.

Whatever purpose Pilate had for scourging Jesus, it did not arouse sympathy from the Jews. Pilate told them a second time: "I find no guilt in Him" (v. 4). Jesus, bloodied and beaten, was now standing before them with a crown and a robe evidencing extreme ridicule, but the Jews still had no sympathy. Instead, when they saw Jesus, they cried out, "Crucify, crucify" (v. 6).

The Insistent Crowd

Pilate told the Jews that if they wanted to crucify Jesus they should do it themselves, and for a third time he declared, "I find no guilt in Him" (v. 6). Pilate refused to respond to the wish of the Jews that he have Jesus put to death without an investigation (18:30). After questioning Jesus, Pilate saw Him as no threat to the Roman government, so there was no reason to put Him to death.

Since the Jews did not want Jesus released, they told Pilate, "We have a law, and by that law He ought to die because He made Himself out to be the Son of God" (v. 7). The Jews referred to the command recorded in Leviticus 24:16: "The one who blasphemes the name of the Lord shall surely be put to death."

Although many people today do not think that Jesus Christ is God, the Jews of His day clearly understood His claim to be God, and this is why they wanted Him put to death. Claiming that God was His Father did not mean that Jesus was inferior to the Father in any way. John 5:18 reveals that the Jews understood from this claim that Jesus was "making Himself equal with God."

Further Questioning
When Pilate heard that Jesus claimed to be the Son of God, he evidenced a new concern. He returned into the judgment hall to ask Jesus concerning His origin: "Where are You from?" (19:9).

Jesus did not answer him, so Pilate asked, "Do You not know that I have authority to release You, and I have authority to crucify You?" (v. 10). Pilate was referring to the authority he had as the Roman governor of Judea. This was a significant government position, and Pilate was understandably impressed with the authority he had because of it.

Jesus brought things into perspective, however, when He told Pilate that he did not have any authority except that which was given to him "from above" (v. 11). The Bible reveals that there is no governmental authority established apart from God's permission: "Every person is to be in subjection to the governing authorities. For there is no authority except from God, and those which exist are established by God" (Rom. 13:1).

A Cowardly Governor
Although the Bible does not record what Pilate thought of Jesus' statement about his authority, it does say that Pilate "made efforts to release Him" (John 19:12). The Jews realized that they had to somehow convince Pilate that Jesu should not be released. They turned their attention from making charges against Jesus and said to Pilate, "If you release this Man, you are no friend of Caesar; everyone who makes himself out to be a king opposes Caesar" (v.12). These words must have struck home to Pilate with tremendous force! Pilate would be in serious trouble if the Roman emperor learned that he was allowing someone to go free who was a threat to the emperor himself.

"Therefore when Pilate heard these words, he brought

Jesus out, and sat down on the judgment seat at a place called The Pavement, but in Hebrew, Gabbatha" (v. 13). Pilate's act was an indication that he was about ready to deliver the sentence concerning Jesus. The Apostle John was careful to pinpoint the time that this took place, for he said, "Now it was the day of preparation for the Passover; it was about the sixth hour" (v. 14).

The Time of Events

There were two ways of reckoning time during the first century. The common Jewish method was sunrise to sunset, a period of about 12 hours. This method of counting time was used by Matthew, Mark and Luke in their Gospels. John, however, writing toward the end of the first century, after the destruction of Jerusalem, used the Roman method of reckoning time—from midnight to noon and from noon to midnight. The "sixth hour" by Roman time could be either 6:00 a.m. or 6:00 p.m. The context of John 19 reveals that it was morning because the trial had been going on during the night. Mark indicated that Jesus was crucified at the third hour according to Jewish time (Mark 15:25); that is, at 9:00 a.m.

So, sitting at the judgment seat about 6:00 a.m., Pilate told the Jews, "Behold your King!" (John 19:14). Perhaps Pilate was only further taunting the Jews before he passed judgment on Jesus. When they again cried out that Pilate should crucify Him, Pilate responded: "Shall I crucify your King?" (v. 15). What the chief priests said at this time is highly significant: "We have no king but Caesar" (v. 15).

It is unbelievable that the Jews would make such a statement. They had chafed under the domination of the Roman Empire for years and had yearned for a king who would deliver them from Rome's oppressive power. But now, because of their hatred of Jesus, they said, "We have no king but Caesar." They seemed willing to stop at nothing in order to have Jesus put to death.

To Golgotha

The Apostle John recorded: "So he then handed Him over to them to be crucified" (v. 16). John went on to tell of the crucifixion, without alluding to many of the details mentioned by the other Gospel writers. John told of Jesus bearing His cross (v. 17) without mentioning that another person was forced by the Romans to carry Jesus' cross part of the way (Matt. 27:32; Mark 15:21). John also told of Jesus coming to Golgotha, or Calvary, where they crucified Him along with two others (John 19:17-18).

So others would know what crime Jesus was guilty of, Pilate wrote a statement and attached it to the cross: "JESUS THE NAZARENE, THE KING OF THE JEWS" (v. 19). This statement was written in three languages—Hebrew, Greek and Latin—which enabled everyone passing by to understand what was written. When the chief priests saw what had been written and realized that it was being read by so many people in the city, they asked Pilate to change the statement to read "but that He said, 'I am King of the Jews" (v. 21). But Pilate refused. Although he had wavered during the trial between the charges of the Jews and the obvious innocence of Jesus, Pilate now stood firm concerning what he had written.

Prophecy Fulfilled

Many prophecies were fulfilled during the few hours Jesus was on the cross. John told of a prophecy that was fulfilled when the soldiers divided Jesus' clothes among themselves while He was dying on the cross. They divided four articles of clothing among themselves, but it was a problem to know who should get the inner garment that did not have a seam (. 23). This was an item of clothing worn next to the skin.

The soldiers decided not to tear the garment but to cast lots to determine who would get it (v. 24). John noted that it was a fulfillment of the Scripture which says, "They divided My outer garments among them, and for My clothing they cast lots" (v. 24). This is a reference to Psalm 22, which prophesies concerning the Messiah, "They divide my garments among them, and for my clothing they cast lots" (v. 18).

Jesus and Mary

Standing near the cross on which Jesus was being crucified was Jesus' mother, Mary. "When Jesus then saw His mother, and the disciple whom He loved standing nearby, He said to His mother, "Woman, behold, your son!" Then He said to the disciple, "Behold, your mother!" From that hour the disciple took her into his own household" (John 19:26-27). The disciple "whom He loved" is commonly considered to be a reference to the Apostle John, the author of this Gospel.

Even as Jesus was on the cross agonizing in death for the sins of the world, He did not forget His mother. He entrusted her to the care of John, which reveals the confidence He had in John. Apparently, the children born to Mary and Joseph after Jesus' virgin birth were not believers at this time or else they would have been the logical ones to care for Mary.

Jesus' Last Words

John drew attention to another prophecy that was fulfilled on the cross. He wrote: "After this, Jesus, knowing that all things had already been accomplished, to fulfill the Scripture, said, 'I am thirsty.' A jar full of sour wine was standing there; so they put a sponge full of the sour wine upon a branch of hyssop and brought it up to His mouth" (vv. 28-29). John was referring to the fulfillment of Psalm 69:21, which prophesies concerning the Messiah, "They also gave me gall for my food and for my thirst they gave me vinegar to drink."

After Jesus had received the vinegar, He said, "It is finished" (John 19:30). This is a highly significant statement because of the tenses John used as he recorded the words of Jesus. John used the Greek perfect tense, which referred to a completed act with a continuing effect. Christ's work of redemption had been completed, and its effect would continue forever. His purpose in coming to earth was to take upon Himself the form of man so He could die on the cross for the sins of the world (Phil. 2:5-8).

No Other Way of Substitution
If there had been another way for people to come into right relationship with God, it would have been unnecessary for Christ to die on the cross. In fact, it would have been a useless death if salvation could come by any other means. The Apostle Paul said, "I do not nullify the grace of God, for if righteousness comes through the Law, then Christ died needlessly" (Gal. 2:21).

Nothing else can deliver from condemnation because nothing else pays the penalty for sin. The Bible declares, "All have sinned and fall short of the glory of God" (Rom. 3:23). But I John 2:2 says concerning Christ: "He Himself is the propitiation [satisfaction] for our sins; and not for ours only, but also for those of the whole world." Because Jesus Christ fully satisfied the demands of God concerning sin, all who believe in Him as personal Savior are delivered from judgment (John 1:12; 5:24).

The Apostle Peter said on the Day of Pentecost, "There is salvation in no one else; for there is no other name under heaven that has been given among men by which we must be saved" (Acts 4:12). The Apostle John said elsewhere in the Scriptures, "He who has the Son has the life; he who does not have the Son of God does not have the life. These things I have written to you who believe in the name of the Son of God, so that you may know that you have eternal life." (I John 5:12-13). These verses reveal that only those who have trusted in Jesus Christ have eternal life, and they also reveal that it is possible for a person to know he has eternal life.

No Broken Bones
In his account of the crucifixion John told about the Jews asking Pilate to have the legs of the victims broken on the cross in order to hasten their death so they could be removed before the Sabbath began (John 19:31). Pilate obviously granted consent because the soldiers then came to carry out

this act (v. 32).

The soldiers broke the legs of the two who were being crucified with Jesus. "But coming to Jesus, when they saw that He was already dead, they did not break His legs" (v. 33). Since Jesus had already died there was no need to break His legs. However, one of the soldiers pierced Jesus' side with a spear, and blood and water flowed from the open wound (v. 34).

John said, "And he who has seen has testified, and his testimony is true; and he knows that he is telling the truth, so that you also may believe" (v. 35). John stressed that he was an eyewitness of these events and that his purpose for recording them was so the reader would believe in Jesus Christ. Again, John emphasized the prophecy that was fulfilled at this time: "For these things came to pass to fulfill the Scripture, 'NOT A BONE OF HIM SHALL BE BROKEN'" (v. 36). John referred to such verses as Exodus 12:46 and Numbers 9:12, which specified that no bone of the Passover lamb should be broken. Inasmuch as the shed blood of the lamb had delivered Israel from Egypt, the Passover lamb pictured Jesus Christ, who shed His blood to deliver all who believe in Him from condemnation.

A soldier using his spear to pierce the side of Jesus was not an act that just happened to occur. John said that this was a fulfillment of another Scripture: "THEY SHALL LOOK ON HIM WHOM THEY PIERCED" (v. 37). This refers to the prophecy of Zechariah 12:10: "They will look on Me whom they have pierced."

It is evident that the crucifixion of Jesus Christ was the focal point of the Old Testament. As one reads the Old Testament, therefore, he should be constantly aware that it is pointing forward to the Lamb of God who came to take away sin from the world.

The Burial

John then told of the burial of Jesus and of the two men who courageously stepped forward and asked Pilate for permission to take care of the body. John said, "After these things Joseph of Arimathea, being a disciple of Jesus, but a secret one for fear of the Jews, asked Pilate that he might take away the body of Jesus; and Pilate granted permission. So he came and took away His body. Nicodemus, who had first come to Him by night, also came, bringing a mixture of myrrh and aloes, about a hundred pounds weight" (John 19:38-39).

Think of the courage it took for these men to identify with Jesus Christ at this time. Their fellow Jews accused Jesus of blasphemy, and this is why they wanted Him put to death, to identify with Jesus, therefore, was to take sides with a blasphemer against the religious leaders. Also, the Roman Empire might not look with favor on anyone identifying with Jesus since He had claimed to be King of the Jews; thus, not giving proper allegiance to Caesar.

No Longer Secret Followers
Although Joseph of Arimathea had not expressed his faith publicly before because he feared the Jews, he now went to Pilate to ask permission to take care of the body of Jesus. The implication seems to be that Nicodemus was also one who had not publicly taken a stand for Jesus until this time.

John 3, which records the conversation of Jesus with Nicodemus, does not indicate what decision Nicodemus made at the time. On another occasion, Nicodemus seemed to be defending Christ when he said, "Our Law does not judge a man, unless it first hears from him and knows what he is doing, does it?" (7:51). Now he came boldly with Joseph to take care of the body of Jesus.

These men had obviously faced tremendous pressure in the past, which had caused them to keep secret their faith in Jesus Christ as the Son of God and the Savior of the world. Although it would have been easy for other believers to have criticized them at the time, at this crucial hour they seemed to be the only Jews who had the courage to come forward and identify with Christ. Many who had been public witnesses for Christ before had withdrawn to a secret witness, but these secret witnesses boldly came forth before the Jewish leaders and the Roman government.

Joseph of Arimathea and Nicodemus took the body of Jesus, wrapped it with linen and the spices they had brought, and buried it in a tomb belonging to Joseph (v. 41; Matt. 27:60). There was not much time to take care of Jesus' body before the Sabbath began, and John added: "Therefore because of the Jewish day of preparation, since the tomb was nearby, they laid Jesus there" (19:42).

The Jewish leaders and Roman officials probably thought that was the last they would hear concerning Jesus. But how wrong they were.

Study Questions

1. Under what circumstances might Pilate himself have considered putting Jesus to death? Why did the Jews consider Jesus worthy of death?

_____

_____

_____

_____

_____

2. What accusation from the Jews against Pilate made him change his mind about Jesus? What claim did the Jews make when Pilate asked them, "Shall I crucify your King?" What is ironic about their response?

_____

_____

_____

_____

_____

3. To discover what specific prophecies were fulfilled during the time Jesus hung on the cross, read the crucifixion account in each for the Gospels, using a good reference Bible. Make a list of the original prophecies and how they were fulfilled at the crucifixion.

_____

_____

_____

_____

4. Why did Jesus entrust His mother to John's care and not to the care of one of His half-brothers? If you have children—or an aging parent—and have no Christian relatives, who would be responsible to care for your children or your parent in the event of your death?

_____

_____

_____

_____

_____

5. Some groups teach that an individual can be saved by doing good works or joining the church or by some other act. If that were the case, then what would be the value of Jesus' death?

_____

_____

_____

_____

_____

6. What happened to the faith of both Joseph of Arimathea and Nicodemus after Jesus' death? Why do you suppose this change occurred? Think of a situation in your life when you knew an action would be unpopular. Was it difficult to take a stand? Why or why not?

_____

_____

_____

Chapter 14 – Our Risen Lord

HAVING TOLD OF JOSEPH AND Nicodemus hastily laying the body of Jesus in a tomb before the Sabbath, John moved on in his Gospel to tell what happened on the first day of the week after the Sabbath.

The Open Tomb

"Now on the first day of the week Mary Magdalene came early to the tomb, while it was still dark, and saw the stone already taken away from the tomb" (20:1). The heavy stone had been rolled in front of the tomb, but as Mary Magdalene approached the tomb she saw that the stone no longer covered its mouth. This caused her immediate alarm. She probably thought that someone had broken into the tomb and stolen or done something to the body of Jesus.

John does not mention in his Gospel what Matthew recorded: The chief priests and Pharisees had asked Pilate to have the tomb guarded so no one could steal the body away and claim Jesus rose from the dead (Matt. 27:62-64). Pilate granted their wish, "And they went and made the grave secure, and along with the guard they set a seal on the stone" (v. 66).

Seeing for Themselves

When Mary Magdalene saw that the stone had been removed from the tomb, she immediately ran to tell someone. She met Peter and "the other disciple whom Jesus loved" (John 20:2), which seems to be a clear reference to the Apostle John himself. She told them someone had taken the body of the Lord out of the tomb. Peter and John immediately ran to the tomb.

Probably because he was younger, John arrived at the tomb before Peter, and "stooping and looking in, he saw the linen wrappings lying there; but he did not go in" (v. 5). Then Peter came racing up and went right by John into the tomb; "He saw the linen wrappings lying there, and the face-cloth which had been on His head, not lying with the linen wrappings, but rolled up in a place by itself" (vv. 6-7). The linen cloths that were wrapped around the body of Jesus were undisturbed, as if nothing had happened. If someone had stolen the body, the cloths would have been taken with the body or scattered around the tomb. The face-cloth had been purposely rolled up by itself and placed a little distance away from the linen cloths. It was evident from these indications that no one had tried to steal the body of Jesus or do anything to it.

At this point John stepped into the tomb, "and he saw and believed" (v. 8). From the evidence, he was convinced Jesus Christ had risen from the dead, although verse 9 says, "For as yet they did not understand the Scripture, that He must rise again from the dead." Although there are Scriptures that refer to the resurrection, the disciples did not understand the significance of what was said. But now at least John was convinced from personal observation that Jesus had risen from the dead.

Jesus and Mary Magdalene

Peter and John returned to their homes, but Mary Magdalene stood outside the tomb weeping (v. 11). As she looked into the tomb, she saw two angels sitting where the body of Jesus had been (v.12). When they asked her why she was weeping, she explained, "Because they have taken away my Lord, and I do not know where they have laid Him" (v. 13).

Having said this, she turned and saw a person she assumed was the gardener, but it was actually Jesus (vv. 14-15). She thought maybe the gardener had carried away the body of Jesus, for she said, "Sir, if you have carried Him away, tell me where you have laid Him, and I will take Him away" (v. 15).

Jesus then said to her, "Mary" (v. 16). On hearing her name she recognized that this was Jesus, her beloved Master.

Why did not Mary recognize Jesus before? Perhaps His appearance was changed to some extent from what it was before His death. It is also likely that since Mary did not expect to see Him, she did not look that closely through tear-filled eyes.

But when she heard her name and recognized that Jesus was alive from the dead, she took hold of Him and clung to Him. Jesus told her: "Stop clinging to Me, for I have not yet ascended to the Father; but go to My brethren and say to them, 'I ascend to My Father and your Father, and My God and your God" (v. 17).

Jesus explained that He had not ascended to His Father. He remained on earth, however, for 40 days in His resurrection body (Acts 1:3). Perhaps Jesus was also emphasizing to Mary Magdalene that His relationship with believers was on a different level than it had been before His death. Whatever the reason, Jesus urged her to tell others, and she went to tell the disciples what she had seen and what the Lord had said to her (v. 18).

Through Closed Doors

That evening the disciples were huddled in secrecy because of their fear of the Jewish leaders. Since the disciples had espoused the cause of the Lord Jesus Christ, the Jewish leaders might try to do away with them as well as Jesus. But while they were hiding in secrecy behind closed doors, Jesus suddenly stood right in their midst (v. 19).

After He had greeted them, He showed them His hands and His side (v. 20). John wrote: "The disciples then rejoiced when they saw the Lord."

Jesus' Representatives

Jesus commissioned the apostles by saying, "As the Father has sent Me, I also send you" (v. 21). Just as He had been the Father's representative in the world, He was sending them into the world to represent Him.

He then breathed on them and told them to receive the Holy Spirit (v. 22). Since the Holy Spirit descended from heaven 40 days later on the Day of Pentecost to take up permanent residence in believers, Jesus' command must have involved the temporary empowering the apostles needed until the Day of Pentecost.

Having commanded this, Jesus said, "If you forgive the sins of any, their sins have been forgiven them; if you retain the sins of any, they have been retained" (v. 23). Was Christ actually giving the apostles the authority to forgive sins? Acts 10:43 reveals that whoever believes in Jesus Christ receives forgiveness of sins.

John 20:23 is better understood when one realizes the Greek tenses involved. The words "have been forgiven" and "have been retained" are in the Greek perfect tense. This tense refers to an action completed in the past with a continuing effect. In essence, Christ was saying, "Whoever's sins you forgive, they have already been forgiven them, and whoever's sins you retain, they have already been retained."

As the Apostles proclaimed the message of Christ, they could also proclaim that whoever believed in Him would have forgiveness of sins because their sins had already been forgiven in heaven. But the apostles could also proclaim that the sins of any who refused to believe in Christ would be retained because they were already retained in heaven. Believers today can announce the same message.

A Doubter Convinced

When Jesus appeared to the disciples, Thomas was not among them: "But Thomas, one of the twelve, called Didymus, was not with them when Jesus came" (v. 24). This verse reveals that the disciples were known as "the twelve," even after Judas had defected. When the ten disciples told Thomas about the Lord's appearance to them, he responded, "Unless I see in His hands the imprint of the nails, and put my finger into the place of the nails, and put my hand into His side, I will not believe" (v. 25).

Eight days later, when Thomas was with the disciples behind closed doors, Jesus again suddenly stood in their midst (v. 26). He invited Thomas to examine and feel His wounds, just as Thomas said he had to do before he could believe (v. 27). This was enough to convince Thomas, and he exclaimed, "My Lord and my God" (v. 28).

What Jesus then said to Thomas is tremendously significant for today: "Because you have seen Me, have you believed? Blessed are they who did not see, and yet believed" (v. 29). Those living in the 21st century do not have opportunity to see Jesus Christ as the disciples did, yet Christ said that those who do not see Him but yet believe are "blessed."

The Bible contains the eyewitness reports of the apostles about Jesus Christ, so the responsibility of each individual today is to believe what is recorded in God's written Word. Believers today do not go on the basis of sight but on the basis of what God's Word says.

Why John Wrote
John then revealed what his true purpose was in writing his gospel account: "Therefore many other signs Jesus also performed in the presence of the disciples, which are not written in this book; but these have been written so that you may believe that Jesus is the Christ, the Son of God; and that believing you may have life in His name" (vv. 30-31).

John revealed that he was highly selective in choosing the material he presented concerning the life of Christ. He made no endeavor to tell everything Jesus did, but what he chose was for the purpose of giving evidence that Jesus Christ was truly the Son of God so people would believe in Him and receive eternal life.

The sole purpose of John's writing his Gospel was not that people might have more facts about Jesus' life. Although John presented many facts, his purpose in presenting them was to cause readers to respond to Jesus as the Son of God by placing their trust in Him. To know the truth is not sufficient in itself; one must respond to the truth. All who respond by receiving Christ as Savior receive forgiveness of sins and eternal life.

Christ's Resurrection All Important

Eyewitness reports of Christ after His resurrection are tremendously significant in establishing the validity of Christianity. If Jesus Christ did not rise from the dead, then His claims of being the Son of God were false. Also, Jesus predicted His own resurrection when he said, "Destroy this temple, and in three days I will raise it up" (2:19). The resurrection of Jesus Christ is proof that all He claimed to be and to do was true.

The Apostle Paul considered the resurrection of Christ to be a central truth in Christianity. The death, burial and resurrection of Jesus Christ, as well as the eyewitness reports, are said by Paul to comprise the gospel (I Cor. 15:3-8).

There were so many eyewitness reports of the resurrected Christ that if one did not believe one of the apostles, he could have gone to others to verify this truth. The resurrection is all important, and Paul emphasized this when he said, "If Christ has not been raised, your faith is worthless; you are still in your sins" (v. 17). But Christ has been raised from the dead, and there were many eyewitnesses to confirm this fact!

At the Seaside

As he told of the post resurrection appearances of the Lord Jesus Christ, John told of the time when Jesus appeared to the disciples at the Sea of Galilee. This sea was also known as Tiberias because of the town on the western shore named Tiberias.

When the disciples were together, Peter announced, "I am going fishing" (John 21:3). The other disciples decided to go along with him, but after fishing all night they had caught nothing, even though some of them were experienced fishermen. They were still fishing when morning came, and from the shore a person called out to them, "Children, you do not have any fish, do you" (v. 5). Jesus asked the question in a way which showed He expected the answer no. The disciples did not know it was Jesus asking the question, but they responded, "No" (v. 5).

He then told them to cast their net on the right side of the ship and they would find fish (v. 6). It was strange that these experienced fishermen took the word of a stranger on the shore, but they did as He suggested and caught so many fish they were not able to draw in the net (v. 6).

John was the first to recognize that the person on the shore was Jesus. He told Peter, "It is the Lord" (v. 7). When Peter heard this, he grabbed his clothes, put them on, and jumped into the water (v. 7). He had his outer garments removed, having stripped himself for work. Although John only says he jumped into the sea, the purpose must have been to get to shore as quickly as possible to be with the Lord because when the disciples later came to shore, Peter was there and helped them drag in the net (v. 11).

When the disciples reached the shore they saw that Jesus already had a fire started and had laid fish and bread on it (v. 9). The word for "fish" is singular, meaning Jesus had only one fish on the fire. Even though Jesus had the ability to bring into existence anything He wanted, He told the disciples: "Bring some of the fish which you have now caught" (v. 10). John specifically states that the number of fish they had caught was 153, and he marveled that with this number of fish the net had not broken.

Jesus called the disciples to come and eat, and John recorded: "None of the disciples ventured to question Him, "Who are You?" knowing that it was the Lord" (v. 12). John noted specifically: "This is now the third time that Jesus was manifested to the disciples, after He was raised from the dead" (v. 14). There were other resurrection appearances of the Lord Jesus, so John must have specifically had in mind the times when Jesus appeared to the disciples as a group.

A Personal Question

After they had finished eating breakfast, Jesus engaged in a discussion with Peter that was highly significant because of Peter's earlier three denials of Jesus (18:17, 25, 27). Jesus asked Peter three times concerning his love. The other disciples were probably aware of Peter's denials of Jesus, and this may have caused tension among them.

When Jesus had predicted that Peter would deny Him three times, Peter had said, "Even if I have to die with You, I will not deny You!" (Mark 14:31). In fairness to Peter, however, it must be noted that this verse concludes by saying, "They all were saying the same thing also." Although the others probably denied Jesus in the sense that they did not take a public stand for Him at this time, Peter was willing to take an oath that he did not know Jesus (Matt. 26:74).

Now that breakfast was finished, Jesus asked Peter, "Do you love Me more than these?" (John 21:15). Although Peter had given the impression previously that his love for the Lord was greater than the other disciples, Jesus was asking him if he was still willing to take that position. In His question, Jesus used the word for the highest form of love (*agapaō*), which refers to seeking another's highest good regardless of the response. This love is not so much an emotional love as it is an act of the will by which one determines to seek the best for the other person. In his answer, Peter did not use this word but a lesser one (*phileō*), which was most commonly used of a friendship.

Again Jesus asked Peter: "Simon, son of John, do you love Me?" (v. 16). This time Peter was not asked to compare his love with that of the other disciples but rather to examine if he truly had love for Jesus. It is one thing to compare oneself with others, but it is quite another to stand alone before God. Again, Jesus uses the word for the highest form of love, and Peter responded with the lesser word when he said, "You know that I love You" (v. 16). After Peter's first answer Jesus told him, "Tend My lambs" (v. 15). Now He told him, "Shepherd My sheep" (v. 16).

One wonders what the other disciples were thinking while Jesus was asking Peter these specific questions. Perhaps Jesus' purpose in interrogating Peter before the others was to let them know that He still accepted Peter as one of His own.

The third time Jesus put a question to Peter, He used the lesser word for love that Peter had been using. Although Peter was grieved about Jesus asking him this the third time, he answered with the same word he had used before: "You know that I love You" (v. 17). This time Jesus responded by saying, "Tend My sheep" (v. 17).

It is difficult to know with certainty all that Jesus wanted Peter to learn from this conversation, but it is evident that He wanted to impress on Peter's mind the need for recognizing one's own nature and also the need to care for those who belong to Jesus. Several years later, Peter urged Christians leaders, "Shepherd the flock of God among you, exercising oversight not under compulsion, but voluntarily, according to the will of God; and not for sordid gain, but with eagerness; nor yet as lording it over those allotted to your charge, but proving to be examples to the flock" (I Pet. 5:2-3). Perhaps Peter was reflecting on the conversation he had with the Lord at the Sea of Galilee when he wrote these words.

Looking to Jesus
After questioning Peter concerning his love, Jesus then predicted how Peter would die. Jesus said, "When you grow old, you will stretch out your hands and someone else will gird you, and bring you where you do not wish to go" (John 21:18). John says that Jesus spoke these words, "signifying by what kind of death he would glorify God" (v. 19). This reveals that the death of a believer brings glory to God. Although God receives no glory from the death of an

unbeliever, the one who knows Jesus Christ as Savior brings glory to God even by his death.

Inquisitive Peter wondered about John, "the disciple whom Jesus loved" (v. 20). Peter asked Jesus, "Lord, and what about this man?" (v. 21). Jesus made it clear to Peter that his responsibility was not to be concerned about John; rather, he should be concerned about following the Lord (v. 22).

Even though Christians are to be concerned about fellow believers, their primary responsibility is to fix their eyes on the Lord and do what He wants them to do.

What Jesus said about John was misunderstood, and a rumor circulated that John would never die (v. 23). However, as the author of the Gospel, John pointed out: "Jesus did not say to him that he would not die, but only, "If I want him to remain until I come, what is that to you?" (v. 23).

Concluding, Important Words

In concluding his Gospel, John said, "This is the disciple who is testifying to these things and wrote these things, and we know that his testimony is true" (v. 24). John was giving an eyewitness report confirmed by others concerning the Person and work of the Lord Jesus Christ.

In order to emphasize how selective he had been in presenting material to confirm the fact that Jesus was the Son of God, John said, "There are also many other things which Jesus did, which if they were written in detail, I suppose that even the world itself would not contain the books that would be written" (v. 25).

This was John's way of saying that it would have taken many, many volumes to record what Jesus did. However, John had been faithful to his purpose that he had set out to accomplish: "These have been written so that you may believe that Jesus is the Christ, the Son of God; and that believing you may have life in His name" (20:31).

Having considered the material that the Apostle John presented, have you believed in Jesus Christ as your personal Savior? If not, even though you may have learned many additional facts about the life of Christ, you are still under condemnation (3:18). However, if you have responded to the truth of the Scriptures and have believed in Jesus Christ as your personal Savior, you have been delivered from condemnation and have passed from death into life (5:24).

Study Questions

1. Make a comparison chart, listing Jesus' followers and how and when they came to believe the truth of the resurrection. Which group or individual demonstrates how you think you might have reacted if you had been there? Why?

_____

_____

_____

_____

_____

2. Some groups teach that John 20:23 gives certain Christian leaders the power to forgive the sins of others. What are the problems with this interpretation, and what would be a better explanation of the passage?

_____

_____

_____

_____

3. What criterion did John use for selecting the material he included in his Gospel? What was his sole purpose for writing?

4. Why is the truth of the resurrection so essential to the teaching of the Gospel?

5. In Jesus' conversation with Peter after breakfast, what was the significance of Jesus asking Peter three times if

Peter loved Him? In what way was each question unique? Suppose Jesus were asking you these same questions today. What would be your response?

_____

_____

_____

_____

_____

6. What specific lessons have you learned from this study of John's gospel? What changes in your spiritual life do you expect to make as a result of this study? Why would you encourage someone else to study the Gospel of John?

_____

_____

_____

_____

_____

_____

_____

Acknowledgments

MANY PEOPLE NEED to be thanked for bringing *John: An Eyewitness Report* back into print.

Thanks goes to Back to the Bible that first published this in 1976 with the same title.

I am indebted to mentors and teachers for giving me a love for the entire Word of God.

Special thanks go to Cornelia Murariu for the cover, Addison Michaelian for helping to transcribe this book, and Renee Fisher for her special enthusiasm in preparing this book for publication on Amazon. I am truly blessed!

About the Author

Dr. Harold J. Berry is a former professor of Bible and Greek at Grace University of Omaha. He served for many years as personal assistant to Theodore H. Epp, founder of Back to the Bible. Dr. Berry holds a Master of Theology degree from Dallas Theological Seminary and a Doctor of Divinity from Grace University.

www.ingramcontent.com/pod-product-compliance
Lightning Source LLC
Chambersburg PA
CBHW031957040426
42448CB00006B/399